Communicating for Change

Roger D'Aprix

Communicating for Change

Connecting the Workplace with the Marketplace

Jossey-Bass Publishers • San Francisco

Substantial discounts on bulk quantities of Jossey-Bass books are available to corporations, professional associations, and other organizations. For details and discount information, contact the special sales department at Jossey-Bass Inc., Publishers (415) 433–1740; Fax (800) 605–2665.

For sales outside the United States, please contact your local Simon & Schuster International Office.

Jossey-Bass Web address: http://www.josseybass.com

 Manufactured in the United States of America on Lyons Falls Turin Book. This paper is acid-free and 100 percent totally chlorine-free.

Library of Congress Cataloging-in-Publication Data

D'Aprix, Roger.
    Communicating for change : connecting the workplace with the marketplace / Roger D'Aprix.
      p.   c.m. — (Jossey-Bass management series)
    Includes bibliographical references and index.
    ISBN 0-7879-0199-7
    1. Communication in organizations.   2. Organizational change.   3. Communication in management.   4. Success in business.   I. Title.   II. Series.
HD30.3.D358   1996
658.4'5—dc20   95–25894

HB Printing   10 9 8 7 6 5 4 3   FIRST EDITION

The Jossey-Bass Management Series

Contents

The most magical connections
are those between the generations,
so I dedicate this book lovingly to
Matthew Michael Sweeney,
the first child of our first child,
Cynthia D'Aprix Sweeney,
and Michael Sweeney.

Preface

The inspiration for this book is my thirty-five years of wrestling with the problem of effective communication inside an organization. For more than twenty of those years I did so at General Electric, Bell and Howell, and Xerox. I was at Xerox for thirteen years, joining the company during its days of explosive growth in the late 1960s, riding its wave of successes during the 1970s, and seeing it go into sudden decline from about 1978 or so until 1981, when I left to become a communication consultant. The Xerox story had a happy ending, and today that story is probably most notable for the fact that the company's leadership stared change in the face and overcame the challenges to the company's survival.

More than a dozen years later, the Xerox story may seem like ancient history. But as one of the first organizations to be buffeted by Japanese competition and to see its market share plummet from more than 90 percent in the early 1970s to less than 15 percent in 1982, it has become an object lesson for any organization that would believe itself invulnerable. In looking at change I believe it is imperative to hold the long view—both of the past and of the future. It is too easy to get lost in the latest fads or quick fixes to significant problems if one does not maintain that long view.

Communicating for Change has been a difficult book to write; when you're personally caught in the tidal wave of change, as I, and countless numbers of workers, have been in recent years, it is hard to maintain your equilibrium and your sense of perspective. Change is both disorienting and puzzling. How do we overcome our inclination to resist it, to deny it, or to continue to rage against it even when its inevitability is clear? That's the challenge for both business leaders and managers of work organizations.

Throughout most of my career in corporate communication and in consulting I have believed that the real challenge in communicating with employees is to create a careful strategy that sees the internal communication process as a system to be managed rather than as a collection of fragmented programs and messages all competing for attention and leaving the employee audience to figure out for itself what it all means. Life in a work organization is too confusing and too complex to permit such a simplistic and, I think, irresponsible solution. If people are to find meaning in their work and to see change as the exciting opportunity it is, they need guidance and leadership from informed leaders who respect them and their contributions. My belief in a strategized communication system rooted in the marketplace is central to everything I say here.

Overview of the Contents

In Chapter One I attempt to provide an overview of the communication problems created by unprecedented workplace change. I state my thesis that the only argument powerful enough to persuade people to embrace workplace change is one rooted in the marketplace.

In Chapter Two I show how people respond to traumatic change, and I outline the principles that leaders must respect if they hope to connect with the members of their organizations. These members are, after all, the people who must make the renewed organization work. I use my Xerox experience here as a metaphor of what organizations face when they begin the change journey.

In Chapter Three I describe the traditional reactive form of communication that has typified leaders' past communication efforts with the workforce. I show through the experience of an imaginary utility what is wrong with that typical effort and why we must find a better way.

In Chapter Four I offer a market-based strategic communication model and show why it is the most logical way to help people connect the demands of the marketplace with their daily work experience. This model is intended to help people make their organizational communication efforts both systematic and proactive. It is both vision and issues driven.

Chapter Five focuses on the critical communication role of leaders at all levels of the organization. I offer a model of that role as a guide to the behavior that leaders must manifest if they are going to help people cope with and connect to change. The model's objective is to build the communication foundation that motivates people to become involved and contribute their best.

Chapter Six concentrates on the all-important role of the senior leader. It outlines his or her major communication tasks and emphasizes the senior leader's role of chief visionary and cheerleader.

In Chapter Seven I attempt to show how the flattening of organizations has made horizontal communication more important than it ever was in hierarchical, bureaucratic organizations. I outline the difficulties of horizontal communication in organizations that are dominated by vertical silos, and end with a discussion of the need to strategize information technology systems so as not to drown people in useless information.

In the final chapter I sum up the essentials of my argument for market-based strategic communication that will allow people to connect their work with the demands of the marketplace.

I have argued for years for a strategic approach to the process of communicating inside an organization. The imperative for that approach has never been more urgent than it is in today's turbulent business environment. In my opinion, the winners in today's global competition will be those who mount a communication system to support all of the other change systems they need in order to succeed. It is no coincidence that in any revolution, the first system the leaders seize is the means of communication—the newspapers, television, radio, anything that they can use to broadcast their messages. We are experiencing a global business revolution. Those "revolutionaries" who ignore the communication system run the very serious risk of not winning the support they need to participate successfully in that revolution.

Acknowledgments

I have not written a book in fourteen years. After working on this one in all of the spare moments I could find in my hectic consulting and travel schedule, I remembered clearly why there has been such a long lapse. Writing is not a spare-time activity. It requires concentration and the ability to remember what you wrote—frequently after a hiatus of two or three weeks or more. As I sat at my laptop laboring over one passage or another, I often felt a twinge of envy for those who had the luxury to do their writing in uninterrupted stages.

As with the other books I've written, my family members were the real victims here. All of that so-called spare time came out of their piece of my life. So, I express most of all to my wife, Theresa, my gratitude for indulging me one more time in a book-writing venture. To my now-grown children who were too young to understand the other books and who read this manuscript eagerly and with great praise, I thank you for your love and support. I dedicated my last book to you and a piece of this one is also yours.

I also imposed on a variety of friends and acquaintances to read different versions of the manuscript. Joan Kampe O'Connor, Dan Koger, and Dave Pincus, among others, were kind enough to offer their comments and suggestions, which is always a courageous gesture—especially when you know that the author only wants to be told how good the writing is and how insightful his ideas are. You were wise enough not to fall into that particular trap. I am grateful for your suggestions and your help.

I want to express my thanks to my editor, Sarah Polster, and her assistant, Barbara Hill. You kept pulling me back to the point and making me say what I meant to say. I am grateful for your insights and your ability to help me stay focused. Change is a moving target, and I hope that I have not missed the mark. We'll see.

I want to thank all of the great people who have taught me so much about communication over the years. My former Xerox colleagues and friends—Tony Francis, John Rasor, Bill Kelly, Hal Tragash, Joe Varilla, and many more too numerous to mention. My communication consulting colleagues at Mercer and Towers Perrin—Jim Shaffer, Mike Emanuel, Richard Bevan, Dennis Roussey, Lea Peterson, Royale Griffith, Bob Seraphin, Marcia Inch, Roy Foltz, Steve Goldfarb, Jeffrey Horn, Rick Anthony, Peter Bugbee, Dan Lupton—you have been a joy to work with.

I owe a special debt of gratitude to the late Father Tom McGrath of the Society of Jesus. He was an inspiration in helping me to understand what real interpersonal communication required from a manager. Much of what I say in Chapter Five comes from his profound influence on my thinking.

And finally a word of thanks to my clients, who have allowed me to learn with them, to collaborate and to develop solutions together.

Here's what I think you all meant.

Rochester, New York   Roger D'Aprix
December 1995

The Author

Roger D'Aprix has long been recognized as one of the seminal thinkers on the subject of strategic communication for companies undergoing significant change. In 1995 the International Association of Business Communicators cited him as one of the twenty-five most influential people in the communication profession in the last twenty-five years. That same organization gave him its highest award in 1978 when it named him a Fellow.

In 1982 D'Aprix wrote *Communicating for Productivity*, which first presented his long-standing vision for making internal communication a planned, strategic process. Both in his work with clients and in the communication profession, he has been an apostle for that strategic viewpoint as well as for the need for organizations to make themselves more hospitable working environments for their people. He is a popular speaker and workshop leader on the subject of communicating change.

In the years since *Communicating for Productivity* was published, strategic communication has become a widely accepted (though not necessarily widely practiced) priority for organizations operating in a turbulent business environment. *Communicating for Change* is an attempt to capture his experience, and the lessons of that experience, during the fourteen tumultuous years since the publication of his last book.

D'Aprix received his B.A. degree in history from Hamilton College, where he was elected to Phi Beta Kappa. He did his graduate work in psychology and counseling. He is a principal of William M.

Mercer, Inc., where he has a long and diversified client list, including General Motors, Westinghouse, Electronic Data Systems, New England Electric, Owens-Corning, Hallmark, and Weyerhaeuser.

D'Aprix and his wife, Theresa, have four adult offspring and a grandson. They live in Rochester, New York.

Chapter One

Turning All Eyes Outward:
The Customer as the Cause of Change

The first question any busy person should ask in browsing through a book like this one is: should I spend my valuable time on this thing, or should I pick up a mystery novel and at least have the pleasure of being entertained and titillated? Let me cut to the chase and tell you exactly what the book is about, and then you can be the judge of whether it's for you, or whether you should just put it back on the shelf.

In writing this book, I had in mind a reader who is convinced that his or her work organization is faced with a compelling need to change if it is to cope with the changing demands of the marketplace. The reader's problem, I assume, is that despite his or her own convictions derived from personal experience, and despite evident conviction at the top of the house, no one is completely sure about how this change will play out. There is more than a little apprehension. There is a heavy dose of uncertainty about the future and how to plan for that future, and there is the nagging fear that the members of the organization—the employees who must make the change work—are not so sure they want to take this particular journey.

Their doubts usually spring from four questions: Is this trip really necessary? Are we up to it as an organization? What will it mean to me and my personal welfare if I stick around? How will I have to change to cope?

A more sobering set of questions comes from that group of employees who see few, if any, choices for themselves. They are the ones who feel trapped in the organization by their long service, their paychecks, and their personal commitments to a way of life or to a particular place. Their questions are: What will happen to me and the people I care about if the organization's leaders can't pull this off? Will I wind up a marginally paid employee of an indifferent work organization in which I see little future? Will I be among those finally counted as expendable?

In their own way, these questions are fully as compelling as any whodunit you could ever choose to read. They are the stuff of personal strife, anger, fear, and suspense. They are also largely unanswerable without reference to a particular person in a particular organization. Therefore, the best I can do is raise them as issues and tell you what I believe you and I need to do to help people through some of their anxiety about change, as well as how to mobilize them in some fashion to make constructive contributions to the cause of changing the organization.

The questions I have cited come to a large extent from the alleged social contract between employers and employees, which people typically interpreted to mean that they were entitled to a job as long as they showed up and performed their work. That contract, if it ever really existed, has been torn up by employers beset with competition and shifting markets, and there is a compelling need to explain to people why that happened and what it means. The answers lie outside the organization in the marketplace that caused the upheaval in the first place. People need those answers if they are to adjust to changing times and regain their bearings at work.

The Ending

I will now violate a basic canon of suspense and tell you the plot of my book. As an author and consultant to organizations in turmoil, I see change not as some dreaded set of awful events beyond our control but as a positive and inevitable force that invites us to share an adventure into the unknown. It is an adventure that we can to some degree shape and control if we keep a sharp eye on its underlying forces, if we think clearly and plan properly, and if we talk to one another about why it's happening, what it means, and how we can cope together. Such talk in organizations is usually called by the all-encompassing term "communication."

So here is my argument in a nutshell:

- Communication is an essential tool for accomplishing change.
- It is a tool that is often used poorly or thoughtlessly.
- To the degree that it is used poorly in organizations, it confuses people. It makes them angry, and it feeds whatever skepticism or cynicism they feel about the motives of the people who lead them—in the process worsening their fears and making them more resistant to change.
- There is a far better way.

Now, before you dismiss this as another homily on the homely virtues of open communication, consider the rest of my argument: the real purpose of effective communication within an organization is to achieve a common understanding of and focus on what the organization is trying to achieve in the marketplace. Because change usually spawns confusion, anger, and skepticism, it requires a powerful rationale to help people understand why they must embrace it. It is not enough to talk about survival, it is not enough to threaten people's livelihoods, and it is not enough—especially today—to appeal to their loyalty.

The only argument powerful enough to encourage people to embrace change is one that is rooted in the marketplace. If the customer insists on change, we have no alternative. To ignore the customer's demands is to make the business irrelevant and eventually insolvent. The trick is to take this reality and convert it into an exciting vision of what together we can become. Most of us want to work and live for issues bigger than ourselves. We want meaning in exchange for all those hours we must spend earning a living.

What we need is a vision of the organization's place in a rational world in order to provide that meaning and to give order and reason to our work lives. An internally focused vision, which often is the knee-jerk response of people in organizations under stress, is doomed to failure. Turning inward is a defense against change, albeit a natural one, because we want to preserve what we have or even return to former glories. But we all know that in the long run an internal focus is an invitation to disaster.

The people who seek, even unconsciously, a return to the old paternalism and a sense of personal entitlement—when generations of families could be assured a job in the company, when careers were cradle-to-grave affairs, and when risk was something to be contemplated with misgiving and reservation—are deluding themselves badly. Their visions are those reflected in a rearview mirror rather than those seen through a window opening on an adventurous world in which people can change, grow, and flourish. The only way we can discourage people from such backward glances is by educating them to marketplace realities. That's true sometimes even of entire organizations faced for the first time with major change.

Connections

Still, few of us can break totally with the past. The basic problem with change is that it tends to sever the familiar and comfortable connections that tell us who we are and what is expected of us. It is important, therefore, during times of turbulent change to establish new connective tissue. I believe that a human being at work is like a mountain climber, who must tether herself to other climbers and in some fashion to the face of the mountain itself. These connections keep her from falling into an abyss. Likewise, whatever logical connections a worker can perceive among the needs of his customers, the strategies of his leaders, and his own daily efforts keep him safe from chaos and alienation.

Poor or absent communication is one of our greatest enemies in the effort to establish such connections. Unfortunately, what often passes for good communication in organizations is the top-down reporting of organizational actions or events. In this approach, the communication task of the organization's leadership is seen as reporting to employees and other stakeholders those actions the leadership proposes to take in response to a given event or circumstance. If there are no events or actions that leaders feel comfortable talking about, there is no communication.

My unscientific observation through the years is that this sort of *reactive communication* is what passes for effective communication in 95 percent of our organizations 95 percent of the time: tell who, what, when, and where; give short shrift to the why. Allow people to draw their own conclusions even if they have little real information on which to base those conclusions. Let them speculate about motives, and give them just enough information to encourage them to invent what they believe is the real story.

The opposite of reactive communication is *strategic communication*, a process by which the leadership of an organization deliberately manages its communications proactively so that they are open, candid, and focused on the marketplace and the customer as the first cause. All of the organization's actions are described as reasoned and logical responses to customer needs and to the forces of the marketplace in which the organization is navigating. And employees are regarded as the critical agents who need information as raw material to inform their own work and to permit them to collaborate with others in supporting a clear and known business strategy.

The Intended Audience

As I wrote this book, I had in mind primarily the three major client groups I usually work with—CEOs and their senior staffs, staff communication professionals, and senior human resource executives. Of course, everyone in an organization that is facing change plays a vital role, but these three groups have key responsibilities—and I think accountabilities—that affect in important ways how the organization perceives and deals with change.

The senior people not surprisingly see effective communication as an important process in making change work to their advantage. They typically want to use communication tools to dispel doubt, to whip up enthusiasm, and to dampen the cynicism and suspicion they fear when they propose fundamental change. They want employees to see the world as they see it from their leadership perspective. Often they are naive about what they believe will or will not work in trying to achieve their communication agendas. They frequently show a predilection for the techniques that good public relations people use to win support from public audiences, who generally have limited stakes in the organization's fortunes, as well as limited firsthand experience with that organization. What senior leaders miss in that predilection is that employees are informed insiders who have a daily basis for comparing leadership words and actions, not to mention an intimate connection to the fate of the organization.

As for staff communication professionals, they often function without adequate access to and support from their own senior management. Some of that lack is structural, having to do with reporting relationships and the like, but much of it is a mutual misunderstanding. Senior leaders too often dismiss their own communication professionals as media manipulators and producers with little understanding of communication as a whole process. Seeing them as producers of media and as innocent of the realities of the business, leaders therefore often decline to ask their counsel on either message formulation or communication strategy.

For their part, professional communicators too often see their management as out of touch, simplistic in their views of how to win employee respect and commitment, and overly interested in appearances at the expense of the truth.

The human resource people in organizations that face the need to change often wind up as leaders or mediators of the organization's change efforts. In the worst-case scenario, their communication views tend to mirror those of the senior leadership, and they cooperate—wittingly or unwittingly—in keeping the communication professionals out of the process. The more likely case is that they do not quite understand how to use the talents and tools that the communication professionals can bring to the party.

Part of my motivation in writing this book has been to encourage all those who are involved in change to view the communication process in the same connected fashion and to see more clearly how they can work together to produce communications that truly match organizational actions with the demands of the marketplace. The three groups discussed here should be the closest of allies; instead, often they have insufficient exposure to one another's thinking and motivation.

A Caution and Some Good News

For those who are enamored with self-help-formula books, I should also make it clear at this point that this is not a classic how-to book. I give short shrift to the ten easy steps or the four simple paths to glory. Change is a complex business that definitely does not lend itself to one-size-fits-all solutions.

Having said that, I will offer you some good news about change. Much of what needs to be done is simply common sense. After years of working to help organizations with communication during times of change, I have concluded that any consultant's major contribution is his or her own broad experience and the ability to help clients break through their organization's inhibiting cultural taboos and limitations to do what they suspected they had to do in the first place. Now, having said that, I will also add that this business of changing whole organizations is damned hard work requiring people to stay intensely focused and to sustain their concentration and commitment in the face of both high ambiguity and high stakes. In

that regard, I must confess that as I have attempted to write a useful book on communicating change I have struggled mightily with
the important issue of how far and how fast an organization can
transform itself. It is tempting to write as though leaders have no
cultural, economic, or historical constraints. One's imagination
can then be given free reign because he is starting with a blank
page. But that's nonsense, because such constraints do exist for real
companies.

There are two further pieces to this issue as far as I am concerned. One is the traditional resistance to change that seems to be
built into the human psyche and that therefore is commonplace in
organizations. It is almost as though each of us comes equipped with
a collection of brain cells whose function is to say, "Wait. Have you
really thought this through? Is this the right thing for you? Will it
work out in the end?" If such cells are there, they are probably the
result of both painful experience and fear of failure. Whatever the
cause, organizational change is usually—in my experience—more
a matter of a series of small and large victories than of overnight
transformation. So, I've written this book with one eye on where
we have come from and on the art of the possible, and the other
eye on where we need to go and on the demands of a fast-moving
marketplace.

Other than relatively new, highly entrepreneurial organizations
with short histories, or those companies that are panicked by short-
and long-term market disasters, I rarely see companies eager to leap
onto the speeding train of change. Most companies usually need a
little time to work up their courage to make that leap, or they hope
in vain that the train will slow down just a bit so they can climb
aboard with less risk to life and limb. However, having acknowledged the reluctance to seek precipitous change, I must also make
the point that incremental change is costly and potentially harm-
ful to the health of an organization. It is a bit like skating over thin
ice. You don't want to linger too long. The quicker you go and the
more deliberate your path, the less danger. The trick is to identify
the change strategies that have the highest potential payback and

the greatest likelihood of success and then to support that change with very effective market-based strategic communication.

The second, somewhat contradictory piece of this issue has to do with the human wish for easy solutions to tough problems. Often when people get past their fear of change, they want to make it happen quickly and painlessly. At that point, they become suckers for the quick fix. In organizations, that wish has usually translated into the familiar fad-of-the-month solution. Everyone knows by now that such simplistic approaches do not work, but often impatience overcomes experience and we opt for what looks like an easy way out.

The particular manifestation of this wish in organizational communication is a history of being program- rather than process-focused. By that, I mean that most of the energy dedicated to communicating change to employees has been directed at the creation of communication programs that looked and felt like tangible evidence that something was being done—and done quickly.

In my view, during times of intense change in organizations not nearly enough thought is given to explaining the why of that change. The explanations are mainly focused on the what, and they tend to be tactical—a print piece of some sort, a video of a talking head, or more recently, a barrage of electronic messages. What people really want to know is why the leadership has taken the action it has.

Historically, the communication profession has tended to be staffed by people I would call craft-oriented. There are many reasons for this (including often their own backgrounds and training, as well as the lack of direct contact with their leadership), but the first inclination of too many of these people is to think of what kind of program or project they should create to transmit the leadership message they hope their management will hand them.

I worry especially about what this means in the information age. There are early signs that communication professionals are following their craft instincts excitedly and uncritically into the wonderful world of cyberspace. Many of them are becoming preoccupied with sophisticated cyberspace technology as an end in itself rather than as a collection of very useful tools. I fear that the admirable goal of keeping up technologically, coupled with their affinity for craft and programs rather than process, may lead them to insufficient regard for message formulation and for clear and thoughtful human communication. The new technology emphasizes speed, timeliness, and volume, three qualities that are not necessarily compatible with clear thinking and careful formulation of ideas and messages. The collective fondness of leaders, communicators, and human resource people for reactive communication makes this a trend worth worrying about.

So, my advice to people charged with making organizational change happen finally comes down to this: in rationalizing change and in mobilizing people's energies, look to the marketplace, read its demands and urgings accurately, and then use your common sense to address what it is telling you to do. In the process, clearly tell employees *what the marketplace is saying to us, why it is saying it, and what we need to do about it together.* In brief, educate them about what they may not know because of their limited perspective. Listen intently to their concerns, their insights, and the early warnings they will provide based on their experience with their customers inside and outside the organization. Engage them in candid and continuing dialogue. Allow them to ventilate their frustrations and anger about having to change, and help them to connect with the message of the marketplace and with one another. If you do so diligently, the change process will be less disruptive and therefore more successful for everyone involved.

The Wrong Audience

You, on the other hand, may come from a place that is very different from the one I occupy. You may wonder what all the fuss is about. You may believe that the world has become a hopelessly more difficult environment than it once was and that the solution is purely Darwinian. The strong will figure out how to cope and later flourish through natural selection and the survival of the fittest. In that worldview, good communication is merely a matter of setting direction and defining requirements that will sort out the fit from the unfit. You may believe further that the unfit will fall by the wayside because they are no longer able to cope with new pressures and requirements, and that all the communication in the world is not going to change that hard fact. The vast numbers of lean organizations in the United States today, created through years of painful downsizings, are ample evidence that you have lots of company.

But my position is that this solution of casting people off is both wasteful and cruel and in the long run perpetuates a brand of workplace resentment that hurts the very productivity the organization so badly needs. If we part company on this important point, this book is probably not for you and you should make tracks to the whodunit section.

Still another reason for instead searching out "Christie, Agatha" in the card catalogue is the conviction that Microsoft, Apple, and other such companies have rendered this whole discussion of top-down, lateral, and bottom-up communication hopelessly anachronistic in the information age. You may have unshakable faith that information technology alone will permit knowledge workers to network purposefully and solve their work problems effectively with little regard for what their leadership does or does not say or do. I do not.

I see these positions as the two extremes of this discussion: what's the big deal—it's merely a matter of adaptation and survival; or what's the big deal—information technology has made the discussion academic. If you don't identify fully with either of these positions, please read on.

How This Book Can Be Useful

My objective is to offer you a mixture of philosophy and practicality. After reading this far, you should now have some idea of the philosophy. The practical part of the book will offer a sounder way to view and support change, as well as a way to understand what is wrong with the way we have been communicating in organizations for many years. It will also offer a simple and logical change model of how to communicate a vision that is connected with the external realities that drive an organization's behavior.

In 1982 I wrote a book that argued for the need to make organizational communication proactive by focusing on the communication of an organization's business objectives and enlisting employee support for those objectives. In the present book, I have taken that basic concept several steps further and have updated it in the context of the dramatic business changes that have occurred since 1982. In the early 1980s I believed that it was both desirable and important to switch from a mainly reactive communication style in organizations to strategic (proactive) communication with employees. In today's turbulent and confusing times, it is not only desirable, it is also imperative if we are to have any chance of winning employee understanding and commitment.

I also attempt to explain what I believe is the still vital but changing communication role of a manager/leader in addressing the communication needs of today's workforce. In the end, I hope that I will have portrayed what I believe—namely, that the workplace is not just a place but a human adventure in which we gather together to accomplish things that are worth our commitment and our energy.

Chapter Two

Enabling People to Connect with Change

A wise senior executive at Electronic Data Systems (EDS) once reminded me of a powerful truth. He said, "Most of us would rather die than change. Think of all of the people you know who still smoke despite the overwhelming evidence that it may kill them. Think of all of us who know we should be watching our diets and avoiding foods that can clog our arteries. Then think of how many of us persist in our behavior because the cost of change is more than we can bear."

So, to talk about *connecting* with change is a revolutionary idea. We are more prone to think about managing change before it manages us. Connecting is a different construct altogether. Our views of change as a phenomenon have a powerful influence on how we perceive and respond to change in our own lives.

Historically, many of us have presumed either that change is cyclical *or* that the present is little more than a culmination of past trends that have led us to our present condition. Both theories are comforting. One tells us simply to wait, that today's experiences have all had their counterparts at some point in human history and when we understand the old trends, the old fads, the new becomes more comprehensible. The new is merely a current repetition of things that have happened before and will happen again in the future. Like fashions in dress, change means the reappearance of old human experiences in new costumes.

The second perspective on change suggests that we can study the past for observable trends that, had we only understood them, would have predicted what is happening now. This perspective urges us to be discerners of present events and to read them to predict the future. Both theories are based on a notion of change as a logical, evolutionary process that flows from the past along a preset course.

A radically different view of change has been proposed by author and scientist George Land in his stimulating and incisive book *Breakpoint and Beyond* (1992). Land and his coauthor, Beth Jarman, argue that change today is an abrupt and powerful break from the past. In their view, change is much more a matter of unpredictable leaps and crucial shifts than it is a linear, progressive series of events all connected to one another. What they call a *breakpoint* is a sharp departure from the past, an event, invention, or insight that carries us far beyond where we had been standing just a moment ago.

In their view, today's global societies are faced with the reality that tomorrow is guaranteed to be nothing like today. The swift movement of technology, the mobility of organizations and people in a global world, the competition for markets and customers have all combined to ensure that the stable, deliberate world so many of us in the developed countries have known is gone.

Organizations and Change

Not surprisingly, many people are both angry and bewildered at the loss. It is as though they have been time-machined into a world they did not ask to join and for which they have had precious little time to prepare. We tend to do our work today in highly developed organizations. Therefore, the rate and character of change in today's world has tremendous implications for the modern work organization and its members.

We often treat work organizations as though they were monolithic collections of like-minded humans, all sharing a common perspective and viewpoint. We speak as though organizations can perceive and manage change according to their own needs and will. And yet, the truth is that any organization is only a collection of individuals, each of whom is very different from the others. Organizations cannot change on their own. They do not in themselves have any capacity for change because they are merely elaborate human inventions created to organize work and to fulfill the human need to belong to something bigger than oneself.

When the climate or culture of an organization does change, it is always because an individual or group of individuals makes a concerted effort to change the organization's direction and character in response to powerful and persuasive market forces. Today's challenge is to determine how such thought-leaders can get the attention of the rest of the organization and persuade its members to understand both the necessity for change and the means of changing. Thought-leaders may or may not be at the top of the organization chart, but what they possess in common is a vision of what the organization must become in a turbulent world.

At this writing, thousands of work organizations throughout the world are wrestling with the fact that their marketplace has changed and that they neither are positioned nor have adequately planned to capitalize on the change. They sense that something is terribly wrong, but in too many cases they do not know how to fix it. And even when they begin to understand what must be done, the challenge they face is to overcome the inertia of the people who either do not recognize the perils they face or are locked in some degree of denial.

Think of IBM in recent times. Think of Kodak and Sears, or any other organization struggling to break out of an old paradigm and create a new one to describe its new marketplace reality. The task is painful, not just because the change itself creates pain, but because organizations that survive the entrepreneurial stage typically move to a stage of consolidating their gains, building a workable structure, and creating policies and methods to protect and grow what they have. It is the movement to that stage of their development that makes them cautious and distrustful of change.

The challenge is to understand and rationalize change and to build the collective will to meet the new opportunities. In the old-line, traditional organization, the process may look daunting at first, but it is really a matter of understanding both human nature and a few principles for communicating change clearly and persuasively. Communicating by itself certainly will not solve the problems, but it is vital in building the consensus that is so essential to successful change. For traditional organizations, change is usually precipitated by significant business problems or even by a threat to their survival.

Fast-growth organizations with an unbroken string of successes face an even more difficult task because it is hard to persuade people to change when the old formula still seems to be working. A bit of American folk wisdom says it all: "If it ain't broke, don't fix it." The problem is that sometimes by the time we discover that it is "broke," it is too late. In both the mature and the fast-growth organization, the enemies of successful change are complacency and arrogance.

Change at Xerox in the Seventies

Consider any company that faces a sea change in its business. Because I was a part of it for thirteen years, the Xerox story of, first, unparalleled growth and then disastrous decline will always serve as a corporate metaphor for me of the plight of today's companies that have it all their own way and then slip into lethargy and near disaster. There is much to learn from the Xerox case, not just because it is a metaphor for the lessons of change, but because Xerox was one of the first American companies to face the onslaught of Japanese competition and the threat that the company's comfortable market niche could be turned into a commodity market with all of the limitations and low growth that implies. Xerox finally faced that change head-on and succeeded in side-stepping the disaster. But in my consulting work, the Xerox experience is never far from my consciousness as I watch concerned leaders trying to understand fundamental change in their businesses.

In many respects the process of change hits the fast-moving, highly successful organization even harder than it does the old-line company that has been through economic downturns in the past, weathered the storms, and emerged whole. The old-line company has learned adaptability, and the lesson that the future can indeed be unkind. The fast-growing organization too often gets seduced into the belief that there is no end to success. The enemy is complacency, which eventually gets transformed into old-fashioned arrogance: "We are so successful because we are so smart and clever."

The trick for the fast-growth company is to maintain a constant air of vigilance and to watch the marketplace for any and all signs of trouble. It is also to educate employees to the market forces that shape company actions and that could derail company success. The trap is to believe that growth can compensate forever for all kinds of inefficiency and the absence of strategy. Eventually, there is a day of reckoning. If the organization has not prepared itself and its people for such eventualities, there is a good chance that change will inflict more pain and loss than it would have if everyone had understood that prosperity could quickly disappear.

Typically, the first reaction to market problems in the fast-paced organization is disbelief, followed by denial. When the leadership of Xerox Corporation found out in the late 1970s that Ricoh in Japan could sell a copier for what it was then costing Xerox to manufacture the same copier, the first reaction was utter disbelief. Once that reaction passed and some thought-leaders began to try to awaken the company to action, the next reaction was the predictable one that *it can't be as bad as people are saying*.

Former Xerox CEO David Kearns says it best in his book *Prophets in the Dark* (Kearns and Nadler, 1992, p. 91):

From a financial standpoint, the early penetration by the Japanese was not all that important, and no alarms went off in our heads. The brisk business we were doing at the medium- and high-ends of the market made the low-end business that most Japanese products were aimed at look trifling. What we failed to grasp sufficiently was that it meant an important toehold for the Japanese. It got Japanese products into American offices where customers could sample them and if they proved to be reliable, come to like them. They were slowly but surely building customer credibility and loyalty.

He then adds: "The important point is that we saw the Japanese coming but did not understand their ability to build good, reliable products at significantly lower cost. It was a similar situation to what American automakers went through. We continually rationalized that we were investing in R&D and that we had plans that would keep us competitive."

Because I was an employee communication manager at Xerox in those days, I remember well the denial and the bewilderment at all levels as the company tried to comprehend the waves of change that were washing over the bow. It was not a pretty picture. But I have since come to learn from my consulting work that such responses are more typical than not.

What happens when people face the awful truth that the marketplace has changed while they have all been busy carrying on the same old activities? How do the members of a work organization face the reality that the competition is not the same old collection of names and logos, but a group of upstarts who either have a new product or service or who have found a way to undercut all of the pricing and leave other organizations in the dust? Or worse, that they were not as smart as they had always thought they were, based on their spectacular track record. Once more, in the words of David Kearns:

Xerox (in the 1970s) was such a fast-expanding and profitable company with such extensive patent protection that a lot of managers began believing their performance as managers was as good as their financial performance. Few Xerox managers were burdened with modesty. And yet at least half the reason for their success was because there wasn't much competition. To sell a Xerox copier was not exactly the world's most formidable task. It was almost as though you were the only person selling milk or the sole heating oil man in town [p. 69].

Stages in Responding to Change

The Xerox case is also instructive in understanding how the members of an organization typically respond to traumatic change. My personal experience in those years taught me that there are distinct stages to that response, and furthermore, that there are clear guidelines one can evoke to cushion the change and rationalize it as the normal workings of the marketplace. We will see later why that rationalization is so important. For now, let's look at the various stages of employee response and then at what I have come to call "market-based strategic communication."

Stage 1. Stage 1 is shock and disbelief. Three questions tend to be predominant in the minds of the members of an organization at this point:

1. How serious are the threats to our organization? (Is this real?)
2. How did this happen?
3. Who is to blame?

This is a crucial, initial step in the process of communicating change because people are trying to understand the personal implications of what has happened. What does it mean to me? Is my job safe? Does the leadership have the stuff to get us out of this mess? If they do not, then what?

At Xerox, market share plunged from an estimated 80 percent in 1976 to 13 percent in 1982 (Kearns and Nadler, 1992, pp. 134–135). In the fading days of the 1970s, panic was only an arm's reach away for most employees. The talk over coffee was a mixture of bewilderment, fear, and hope. And in truth, it was all compounded by poorly thought out and poorly executed layoffs that went on during 1981 and 1982 like Chinese water torture.

Stage 2. Since those days, I have seen countless organizations make the same mistake as they bought time by cutting the workforce while they figured out what to do next. The question on the minds of most Xerox people in 1981 and 1982 was, "Do we have a plan of action? If so, what is it?" That question signifies Stage 2, which comes hard on the heels of Stage 1. The most frightening suspicion for any employee group is that there is no battle strategy, that the war will be only a series of firefights in which people will be picked off one by one as the generals try to concoct a strategy on the spot.

Stage 3. Stage 3 is characterized by the natural human desire to want to do something to solve the problem. Its hallmark is another question, namely: What do you want me to do? How can I help? When people reach Stage 3, someone better be able to answer their question or they are likely to be demoralized by their helplessness.

Critical to both the management of change and the communication of change is a visible strategy anchored in the realities of the marketplace. Once that strategy has been identified—even if it is only a rudimentary response to the organization's plight—it is imperative to begin offering it to the workforce as a means of mobilizing them, particularly if they have reached Stage 3 in their response to events.

In the very early 1980s, Xerox was gripped by the kind of angst I am describing. In the years since, hundreds of other global organizations have replicated the Xerox experience, largely because they were caught off guard by fundamental change in their markets.

Once the leadership has sketched a basic strategy they will use to address their plight, they must recognize that the organization has become an environment full of mixed signals, fear, and what in broadcasting would be called "noise and clutter."

Employee Response to the Threat of Change

The challenge is to break through the noise and clutter. If we understand Stage 3, we have a strong clue on which to base future action. When people ask what our plan is, they are really asking much more. Figure 2.1 shows roughly how people respond to a claim by the leadership that the organization must be transformed.

At one end of the curve are the few people (10–15 percent would be a reasonable estimate based on my experience) in the organization who are afflicted with an abiding anger. They are usually the ones most heavily invested in things as they are, or they are the poor souls who cannot abide change in any form. Either they wish to blame someone in the leadership and see that person punished for what they regard as his or her neglect of the business, or they want things to be the way they were in the good old days.

**Figure 2.1. Likely Employee Reaction
to Announced Corporate Transformations.**

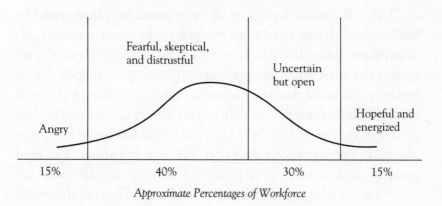

Approximate Percentages of Workforce

At the other end of the curve are those few (again, about 15 percent based on my experience) who are energized by the admission that things have gone sour and that drastic action is necessary. They are usually the people who read the warning signs sooner than the rest and conclude early on that something must be done or the enterprise will be in serious trouble.

At Xerox, we had both types of people. One of the heroes of the hopeful and energized group turned out to be an unassuming and extremely bright psychologist who had held a variety of staff positions in Human Resources. His name was Hal Tragash, and he was the persistent soul who faced down the opposition to change by virtue of his belief in people and in rational response to difficult circumstances. Tragash was the prime mover, under Dave Kearns's leadership, in seeking employee involvement in addressing the monumental problems the company faced as it tried to invent a new strategy to save the business.

In these days when self-managed work teams and total quality management programs are commonplace practices, it may not seem particularly revolutionary to turn to the workforce for their ideas and solutions, but in 1981, employee involvement was far from a tried and true technique. In fact, the skeptics were everywhere. Tragash's great accomplishment was to win the begrudging consent of the skeptics at Xerox to try his ideas, which to that point had rarely been implemented, to help turn around a troubled organization.

The bulk of the employees in any organization threatened by fundamental change usually fall into one of the two remaining positions on the curve shown in Figure 2.1. The majority (about 40 percent of the total employee population) are fearful, skeptical, and basically distrustful that the leadership has built a strategy that will work. Their skepticism is usually voiced quietly and soberly as they gather in groups of two or three to critique the latest efforts to change the organization's direction and even its culture. The final group of employees (about 30 percent of the total) are those who are uncertain but who are basically open to change. They are the crowd who say: *Let's give them a chance. Wait and see. This could work!*

Guidelines of Market-Based Strategic Communication

It is important to understand this basic organizational mind-set and the noise and clutter behind it, because it is this mind-set that begins to suggest the communication actions that must be taken to move the curve from the left and tilt it increasingly to the right. Once the elements of a responsive strategy are in place, the following steps may be taken to make communication not only strategic but also market-based:

1. *Create and communicate a clear and simple case for change, based on market and customer realities.* The logic here is that you are asking people to accept the need to change their personal and group behavior. Most of us hate that kind of change and will resist it unless we recognize a compelling case to embrace it. That case can only be made in terms of the realities of the customer and the forces that are currently driving the organization and that are likely to drive it for some time to come.

2. *Clearly identify and communicate the market forces that the organization faces in doing business.* These are the root causes that will drive change for the foreseeable future. To do their jobs, people must understand these causes so they can align their work activities and habits with the needs of the customer. What is clearly missing in so many contemporary organizations is context—*the larger picture that captures the plight of the organization and rationalizes its behavior.*

3. *Formulate and communicate a responsive business plan.* The great frustration for so many people in the trenches is that at some level they do understand what the organization faces because they are dealing with it or hearing about the real-life experiences of their peers and colleagues. What these people need is the conviction that their leaders have grasped the problems and are moving to address them with a reasonable plan of action. Unfortunately, too much of what they see is focused only on cutting costs and eliminating people. Common sense tells them that much more is needed than that simplistic approach. The advocates of corporate secrecy often argue

that any disclosure of strategy or direction to employees will give aid and comfort to the competition. What they overlook is that the competition most likely has an intelligence pipeline into the organization anyway, and that the only people being kept in the dark are those who have to make the new strategy work.

4.   *Outline the consequences of success and failure.* Here the goal is to inspire hope and, frankly, to raise the specter of what could happen if the problems went unaddressed. At this point, an inspiring vision can be a tremendous visual aid for a group of people who see more confusion and bewilderment than they like. I will say more about vision later, but for now it is important to understand how exciting and hopeful a truly inspiring vision can be for people struggling to understand and cope with fundamental change.

5.   *Finally, tell and retell.* Many people who rise to positions of leadership and power are impatient souls with brief attention spans. If they are going to ready their organizations for change, they absolutely must inhibit their impatience to move onto the next subject and to stop talking about the marketplace and the strategy needed to succeed in that marketplace. Leadership has much to do with providing a constant focus. The mortal enemy of that focus is leadership impatience and the desire to talk about other things.

This act of repetition distresses both the managers and the staff people charged with providing message reinforcement through the organization's official internal channels. They think that somehow this repetition bores people and saps their ability to listen. If it is not done creatively and with some passion, that is certainly true. But it seems to me that the real challenge for the professional communicators, including line managers, is to breathe new life into the key issues and messages and to find new variations on what they incorrectly believe are all-too-familiar themes. As many observers have pointed out, when the communicators are sick of saying the same old things, that is probably just about when the message is beginning to connect with the audience; so the trick is to find yet another way to say it so it will truly take hold.

All of these guidelines are aimed at communicating change to a distracted, unsettled employee audience. They are not a panacea that will make everyone thrilled about the need to change personal work habits and priorities. Further, they are certainly not something that can be instituted temporarily in an organization and then abandoned. The long-term challenge is to make internal communication a market-based strategic process, influenced by the principles of continuous improvement.

The Xerox Lesson

I have used my Xerox experience here as a metaphor for the change cycle. Armed with 20/20 hindsight, I can now see the important communication flow that occurred with the change at Xerox. In late 1981 I despaired that the leadership was going to fulfill its communication obligations to the workforce, so I left, feeling that if I could not influence the free flow of information, I had no business staying in a job that I thought required me to do exactly that.

The company's tradition was that of a relatively open though sometimes bruisingly political culture. In the early stages of its fear and panic in 1981 and 1982, it forgot the communication lessons of the past and chose to say little to employees about its intentions and plans for the future. Some of that initial reluctance was perhaps understandable. The strategy was still unborn, and no one feels like talking when the bottom seems to be dropping out of the world or when it is unclear if the free fall can be halted.

David Kearns has admitted that in 1982 he had private doubts about whether the company would survive the 1980s or be sold off in a fire sale and closed down by 1990 (Kearns and Nadler, 1992). But once the company regained its bearings and charted its direction, to the credit of Kearns and the rest of the leadership, effective communication became the underpinning of the quality strategy used to save the company.

The ultimate lesson of the Xerox case history was the ability of the leadership to establish connections between the company's plight and the rational solution of orientation to customers and quality as the way out of the mess. Using the marketplace as the first cause of everything, Xerox senior management mobilized the workforce to focused and constructive action. It was not a particularly neat process, nor was it especially clear-cut. Much was invented by the players as they acted to restore the company to good health. The ultimate conclusion was that the race would never be won, that, in David Kearns's words, it was "a race without a finish line."

Reconnecting

In the end, the notion of connections is critical to any organization facing serious change. The basic problem with change is that it destroys connections—between an organization and its customers, between market forces and business strategy, between ourselves and our organizations, and even among employees within the organization.

Xerox ultimately succeeded in its struggle because it used the total quality process as a vision of how the company could reconnect itself to all of its life support systems. It justified its choices in terms of the common cause that all organizations share—namely, serving customers and the marketplace.

While everyone believes in effective organizational communication in theory, many have strong reservations about it in practice. The reservations usually stem from a basic fear that people cannot handle change, or even the truth about their lives, that they are like children who need to be protected from the truth. Without trust in human nature, there can be no communication.

For those organizations that truly are willing to confront change, the imperative is somehow to rise above the ugly notion that people cannot be trusted. Then, and only then, we can begin to construct the all-important visions that give hope to our work and meaning to our lives. That, in the final analysis, is our best strategy for absorbing and managing fundamental change in the workplace.

Let's look next at how we typically mishandle change communications, and then see what we can do about it.

Chapter Three

The Pitfalls of
Reactive Communication

Few leaders in today's workplace would deny the importance of effective communication as a tool for accomplishing change. Their problem usually is not knowing where to start, or even finding the time in their overburdened schedules. Believing that they do not have the time, and bombarded with conflicting pressures and demands, many of them tend to use their communication tools poorly.

Their various advisors—whatever their job responsibilities and reporting relationships—tend to get caught in the same net. There is time to make decisions and to act on them—not to explain them. The actions will have to speak for themselves.

The trouble is that actions rarely speak for themselves. In the end, this is a dangerous game that leaves workers confused, angry, and skeptical. Indeed, in my own work interviewing all kinds of workers in myriad organizations caught up in difficult company changes, I am increasingly struck by the rising levels of employee anger and distrust. Overwhelmed by unexplained change, they revert to the belief that management has no respect for them or no use for them beyond the present, short-term requirement for their labor.

Compounding their reaction is a change in the social contract—a radical change that has largely gone unexplained in the workplace—which they believed gave them lifetime employment in exchange for their loyalty and their mere presence. Workers have mostly concluded on their own that the social contract is no longer in force, but they don't have anything to replace it with. So they revert to a sense of betrayal and unfocused anger, not to mention denial of the realities around them.

Given a world in which employees are increasingly counted on to produce quality products and supply quality services to demanding customers, employee anger is not something to dismiss lightly. The likeliest scapegoats for employees' repressed anger are the very customers they must serve. If you doubt that, think back to your personal experiences with surly service from indifferent service providers. You were their only safe target.

What Is Reactive Communication?

I have already stated my educated guess that the vast majority of leaders of work organizations communicate reactively 95 percent of the time, at great cost to themselves and to their organizations, but that cost is largely hidden and therefore discounted.

Why reactive communication is so prevalent is not hard to understand. In its simplest form it is the normal human experience of telling people what we have seen or heard. We all carry on this kind of communication routinely, as we recount our own experiences to our fellow humans. It is so familiar that it seems like the logical way to behave. We experience an event, and we recount it.

The trouble is that when we bring this style of communication to the workplace, we find ourselves in a complex social environment riddled with personal competition, ego, and distrust. No longer is the transaction a simple matter of recounting an event to an interested and trusting listener. Now we have lines of authority and divisions of responsibility to consider. There are turf boundaries carefully guarded by people who identify their interests closely with their functions and their positions in the organization. And there are cultural taboos about admitting mistakes, acknowledging personal shortcomings, or showing vulnerabilities. In short, the situation is fraught with difficulties, and people learn when to talk and in whom they can safely confide.

To make matters worse, most official reactive communication in the workplace is written. We forget that in our normal reactive transactions with other people the message is usually delivered face-to-face, with the opportunity for questioning, reading facial expressions and body language, and detecting inflections in voice. Not so in organizations. The typical reactive communication is written, formal, and delivered impersonally. Typically, the audience believes—usually correctly—that the message has been carefully crafted and reviewed to remove any hint of humanity. Obscured by officialese and passive-voice expressions to avoid fixing blame or responsibility, the message often ends up as an object of scorn and ridicule.

Bad news has typically been sugarcoated both down and up the chain of command. The language has been selected for just the right nuance and connotation. And the timing of message delivery has been rigidly determined so that it arrives at a time to control its impact—ironically with little regard for urgency or timeliness. Anyone who has ever worked within a hierarchical power structure with status-sensitive and egocentric leaders is familiar with the problem.

Reactive Communication in Action

To understand fully the pitfalls of reactive communication, consider the following real-life scenario at an electric utility I'll call All-Purpose Gas and Electric. CEO Gerard Power, has convened his senior staff on a Monday morning to announce that declining earnings are more than a straw in the wind. He wants their support for a 15 percent cut in the workforce over the next three months. After prolonged discussion about how best to achieve Power's target, the staff concur and agree to develop an action plan ASAP. At the close of the meeting Power swears them all to secrecy, lest the word get out and upset morale and productivity.

The reactive model shown in Figure 3.1 shows what typically happens next. Remember that the key to reactive communication

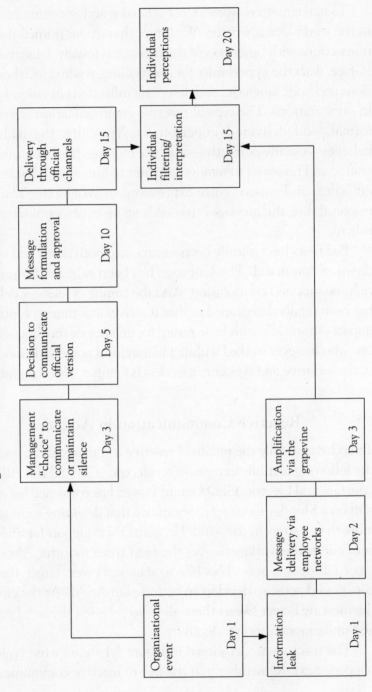

Figure 3.1. Model of Reactive Communication.

is "no event, no communication." The event in this case clearly is the proposed downsizing action which for now is to be kept secret from All-Purpose employees.

On that landmark Day 1, represented by the box on the left side of the figure marked "organizational event," All-Purposes's treasurer Frank Deficit leaves the senior staff meeting and walks glumly into the office of Eberhard Gooch. He shuts the door quietly and breaks the news to his trusted assistant with one immortal admonition.

"You've got to promise me," he says conspiratorially, "that you will say nothing about this to anyone. Not even your wife, Gloria." When Gooch agrees with a vigorous nod of his head, Deficit tells him the whole story as it unfolded that morning at the staff meeting. Deficit knows that he will need Gooch's help to develop the early retirement package that All-Purpose would offer to cushion the cutbacks, so he believes that he has no choice but to establish this confidence.

On Day 3, the senior staff meets again, and Power revisits briefly the earlier decision not to communicate the downsizing action yet. He wants reassurance that this is the correct tactical decision at this point. Everyone agrees that the loss of productivity that would follow any such announcement would be devastating. "We will keep this under our hats," says Deficit to the assembled group. "Does everyone agree?"

Unbeknownst to Deficit, on Day 2 Gooch had already decided to confide in his trusted assistant, Muriel Loostalk, so that she could clear her calendar for the work crunch that would ensue in formulating the early retirement package.

On Day 3 when the senior staff is vowing to keep the news under their hats, Loostalk visits the cubicle of Gerry Telafriend, one of her best friends in Engineering. Peering discreetly over the low partition wall, she confides to him that there is going to be a layoff soon. He promises to keep her secret, although in fact he has heard a rumor from a lineman whose stockbroker had given him a security analyst's report on emerging competition in the utility industry.

All-Purpose was cited as one of the most vulnerable utilities, caught in an earnings squeeze because of its high overhead costs. The analyst had commented that he could not see how All-Purpose could avoid layoffs in the near future.

As soon as Loostalk leaves, Telafriend is on the phone to all of his colleagues to drop the bombshell he has just heard that confirms the earlier rumors. The next day, while standing at the washroom sink, public affairs director Ed Nuisman is aghast to hear two accountants quietly recount that a layoff is planned for two weeks hence. Their version calls for a 20 percent cutback that will mainly hit union employees in three states. According to one of them, everyone over age fifty-five will be vested with at least partial retirement benefits if they accept the package.

It is now Day 5. The senior staff convenes for its weekly meeting. Nuisman recounts the conversation he overheard the previous day and argues forcibly that the Public Affairs department should be preparing a communication package for the media as well as for security analysts because this is going to get out . . . if it hasn't already. Someone wonders if an employee announcement is now in order. Power blanches at first, as he contemplates the lost employee productivity, but he finally agrees that it may be a good idea.

Nuisman picks up on the issue of how to break the news to employees. He wants employees to be informed at a series of face-to-face meetings. Company attorney Fred Kautious warns the staff that such meetings would expose them to difficult and embarrassing questions for which nobody has definitive answers and that the meeting content will surely leak both to the press and to financial markets.

After extensive discussion, Power informs the group that essentially he agrees with both Nuisman and Kautious. The answer, he says, is a well-worded press release that will go simultaneously to the media and to employees so that everyone gets the same message at the same time. He instructs Nuisman to begin writing the release immediately so that senior staff can review and approve it.

By that evening, Nuisman has the release ready to go into the approval mill. On Day 10, after constant wrangling with one staff member or another over word choices, he finally has all of the staff revisions. Frank Deficit insists that he remove any specific mention of a possible impact on earnings. Human Resource director Peter Pander wants stricken any breakdown of affected employees by job category. Attorney Kautious scrawls, "Have you lost your senses?" beside the comment, "The company is making every effort to place affected employees both inside and outside the company—especially our older long-service employees." Marketing director Mike Hustler reminds Nuisman that "our competitors will take every advantage of this announcement. Can we limit it only to the local news media?" Power rewrites every sentence in the passive voice to soften the impact of the decision.

On Day 15, the employees finally receive a special E-mail version of the heavily reviewed and approved announcement as a memo from Gerard Power.

Here is a sampling of what happens next:

• Local TV anchors appear at All-Purpose work sites to interview exiting workers as they finish their shifts. Those who will talk on camera express their disgust with the announcement and the greed of All-Purpose management in seeking higher profits at the expense of long-service employees. They comment that everyone is devastated and thinks that this is only the beginning. One union steward is particularly vehement when interviewed at his truck with the All-Purpose logo gleaming in the afternoon sun.

• A highly speculative newspaper account appears in the local newspaper, complete with anonymous and unflattering speculation from disaffected employees about management's motives and intentions. Comments from the news release are used only as background for words like, "The company has alleged that. . . ." The official version says, "One of the most jarring quotes back at All-Purpose headquarters is, 'We find this necessary action painful, but we see no choice,' says highly paid utility official Gerard Power.

Power," it continued, "is reputed to be one of the highest paid CEOs in the utility industry."

- Two New York security analysts say that the action shows "disappointing financial problems at All-Purpose that heretofore had not been revealed." They cautiously advise investors to monitor the situation carefully during the next few months.

- The bargaining agent for the union blasts Pander and All-Purpose for lack of advance notice and for arousing unnecessary fear among union members for their jobs.

- Over the next several weeks employee productivity nosedives as people speculate over dozens of possible scenarios for the final cutbacks.

- A previously scheduled employee survey is administered between the announcement and the actual layoff, and results show that employee morale levels have reached a new low as have trust of management and concerns about the future of jobs at All-Purpose.

Underlying Assumptions

Is this a far-fetched scenario showing the worst-case results of bad communication 1950s style? Not really. It is a drama we still see played out almost daily by companies that decidedly should know better. If you doubt that, watch the daily business pages of your favorite newspaper. In an era of downsizing and uncertainty, with few clear answers to difficult questions, company leaders too often revert to noninformative explanations that show little regard for people's information needs, intelligence, or emotional welfare. In the 1980s and 1990s, we have become so accustomed to such scenes that we perceive them as just another indication of the changing workplace and its unrelenting impact on people's lives. What we often do not realize is that much of this could be avoided if it were not for our collective cavalier attitude about human communication needs at work.

The humane argument that leaders owe people information that affects their lives and personal fortunes often carries little weight in these days of pit-bull capitalism. So, let's put aside for a moment the philosophical and ethical need to treat people like dignified human beings, and review the logic underlying the All-Purpose case. At least two key assumptions are at work.

Assumption 1 is that premature release of information could hurt both employee morale and productivity. The rest of the syllogism goes about like this: we can ill afford declining morale and productivity; therefore, we will not communicate with employees until we decide the time is right.

Assumption 2 is that release of negative news outside of the company could hurt the company's reputation with various constituencies that are important to it. The rest of this syllogism goes like this: certain constituencies (such as shareholders, community leaders, customers, security analysts, and so forth) may be upset by this negative news; therefore we will do our best to manage the release of the news in such a way that we minimize its impact.

In both cases the resulting strategy is to communicate either close to the vest or not at all. It is also to wait until events are very clear and can be reported as accomplished facts. It would seem that anyone who ever studied Watergate and the forced resignation of Richard Nixon or who has seen one or more corporate leaders squirming under the television lights to explain their version of their *Exxon Valdez* episode would know better. But the lesson is one we never quite seem to absorb except in a few isolated incidents that become famous because they are exceptions. The Tylenol crisis—in which Johnson and Johnson unhesitatingly recalled potentially contaminated Tylenol capsules and took every possible step to protect the public interest—comes immediately to mind as a positive handling of a tragic event.

A Litany of Shortcomings

So, aside from leaving the communication task mainly to the grapevine, what else is wrong with reactive communication? Here is my litany of shortcomings.

Why? and What Does It Mean?

First, reactive communication focuses mainly on the *what* when the question people really want an answer to is "Why?" or "What does it mean?" The what of any event is usually pretty straightforward, for example: the plane crashed into a mountainside. It may be possible to elaborate a great deal on that simple fact, but it all comes down to a plane crash. What we often have to wait weeks and months to find out is *why*. Why did it happen, and what can we learn to prevent similar events in the future?

In the workplace the easiest thing to find out is the what. The employee grapevine will be full of the themes and the subtext of the what, with a fairly complete list of prospective heroes, villains, and victims. But what inevitably is missing—regardless of the accuracy of the grapevine information—is a solid explanation of why, and what the whole thing really means in the long run.

Some lack of information is natural because corporate leaders do not always have complete answers to every question early on, and they have been taught to keep their mouths shut when they do not have all the answers. Some of the reluctance to communicate also stems from the ridiculous belief that the leader must be all knowing and always in control of events; but such omniscience is impossible, and it is therefore a myth we need to put to rest.

The good leader in the twenty-first century organization must be able to acknowledge ambiguity and not be afraid to speculate intelligently from what is known. That speculation may turn out to be off the mark, but it is certainly better than leaving people to draw their own conclusions from bits and pieces of information they find on their own.

We have taught one another above all else to fear being wrong. What we forget is that we seldom hold people accountable for their predictions of the future. If we did, economists would be fearful to project trends, futurists would keep their visions to themselves, and astrologers would be an endangered species. Does anyone but leaders themselves believe that people expect leadership omni-science in the first place? I doubt it.

The Say-Do Conflict

Frequently, the final result of reactive communication is a mixed signal. We say one thing and then do another. The "Say-Do" con-flict in organizations is enough to drive people crazy. Indeed, a matrix can easily be developed with the *Say* dimension on the ver-tical axis and the *Do* dimension on the horizontal axis (see Figure 3.2). Ideal communication within the organization is characterized by a leadership that matches its words to its actions—such an orga-nization could be called a High Say/High Do organization.

The worst position on the matrix is High Say/Low Do. In such organizations, no one trusts or believes the leadership anymore. Communication is all talk and no action, and it offers a mixed sig-nal that people finally read as a lie.

The Low Say/Low Do portion of the matrix is typically less of a problem, unless employees perceive a lingering problem or a future danger that no one is acknowledging. In that case, the oversight can be very disturbing.

The last of the mixed signals is Low Say/High Do. This one is tricky. Employees want to know: do you not tell me because you do not want me to know? Do you hold back your comment because your actions should speak for themselves? Or do you simply think that the issue is not worth talking about? And if that is the case, why do you spend so much time acting on it?

Two Views of Leadership

The next two limitations of reactive communication are inter-twined. Such communication causes people to speculate on the cause of an event because they need closure. Unexplained and uncommunicated events rouse their curiosity and unsettle them.

Figure 3.2. The Say-Do Matrix of Organizational Communication.

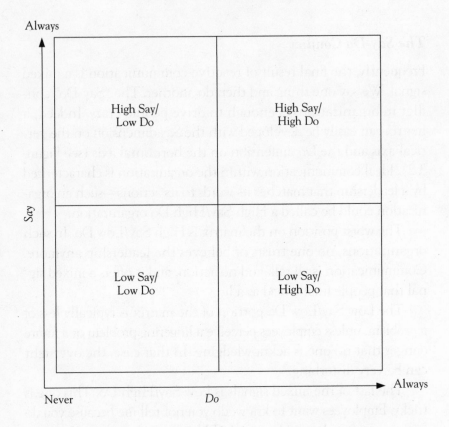

They will inevitably fill the void with grapevine explanations. But—and this is a critical but—their explanations will only be as good as their ability to deduce leadership motivation by reasoning back from the event. What a monumental task!

How do employees understand the motivation behind All-Purpose's cutbacks unless Mr. Power tells them what circumstances have led him to this action? Presumably, he is a rational man who has weighed the alternatives and come to a rational decision. Why not tell people what those alternatives were and why he selected the one he did? Is there a hazard to that kind of disclosure? Evidently there is or there would be much more of it. But how much greater the hazard to let people guess.

In my experience, people have two theories of leadership. You will recognize both almost immediately. The first one is the conspiratorial view. It goes like this: "Mark my words. You heard it here first. *They know exactly what they're going to do.* You'll come back here next week and tell me that I was right on the money. This is part of a grand plan, and this is only the first phase. It's 250 people this time. Next time it will be at least twice that number, and then who knows?"

In the mind of the speaker there is a full-blown conspiracy underway, with management knowing all the details but unwilling to reveal any of them. The assumed motivation is simple: "They don't care about us, and they're only taking care of themselves." I would bet my last nickel that every one of us has been a party to this kind of discussion, willingly or otherwise.

The second view of leadership is what I like to call the Curly, Larry, and Moe theory. It goes something like this. "Oh, my God! We are in deep trouble, and those guys don't have a clue. How come I can see this at my level, and they still don't get it? Where is our strategy? Where is our battle plan?"

All too often the members of an organization retreat to this position when they see little or no evidence of action in the face of adverse circumstances. When Xerox was in difficult straits in the late 1970s, we commissioned an employee research study to see what sorts of communication issues faced us. The results were instructive.

In individual interviews with our consultant, Mike Emanuel of Myron Emanuel Communications, each of the senior leaders said the same thing: "We have competition for the first time, and our people don't understand how serious things are or how bad they might get." The senior leaders were unanimous in their view that employee apathy and complacency were the common enemies along with aggressive competitors.

When Mike interviewed our people in the trenches in focus groups, he got an entirely different story. One of the replies to his question about the toughest issues facing Xerox at the time is a favorite story of mine. "This is the first time," the employee began, "that this ship has ever been in heavy seas. And all of those turkeys in management are hanging over the side."

Besides the deliciously mixed metaphor, what came from the group was the deep concern that it was getting harder and harder to sell the copying machines on which we had held a virtual monopoly until that time. Their worry was that there was no strategy, no plan in place to cope with the adversity that was buffeting them every day in trying to do their jobs.

Through the years, I have come to believe that the conspiracy theory, with its impugning of management as mean spirited, is perhaps less damaging than the Curly, Larry, and Moe view of life, with its clear sense of one's vulnerability to incompetence in high places. Regardless of which is more damaging, choosing one of these views over the other is a painful choice. The real answer is to stop pretending that reactive communication works in an organization.

Information Overload and Diffusion of Responsibility

Two other consequences of reactive communication as the normal mode of leadership are information overload and the diffusion of communication responsibility. In the organization that relies chiefly on a communication strategy of reacting to events, it is inevitable that people will suffer when they receive bits and pieces of information that they cannot assemble into any coherent whole. There is no perspective, no context, no clear frame of reference on which they can hang the events of their work lives.

In an era of instant communication technology, this problem is worse than it has ever been before. E-mail, the fax machine, voice mail, and the informal information networks each of us has all combine to provide people with information they cannot easily process.

The result is that at some point, they must shut down to protect themselves from overloading their personal information circuits. How they do that is a highly individualized response based on prior experience and personal beliefs, but the consequence for the average worker is a sense of chaos and a feeling that things are out of control.

The final negative effect of reactive communication is a diffusion of communication responsibility in the organization. If the leadership appears to be reluctant to speak honestly about what is going on or to attempt to control the delivery of information according to their own agenda and timing, it is no surprise that people in lower leadership positions emulate that behavior. Why should they stick their necks out if it is so clear that the leadership is afraid to communicate? Their defense is a simple, "I only work here." No one should be surprised that supervisors and the like are wary communicators in any organization that chooses to communicate reactively most of the time.

In today's information society there are hopeful signs of a new willingness to share information more honestly and in a more timely fashion inside the organization. But that willingness will not be translated into anything constructive until we are clear about what works and what does not work in leading a workforce.

As I have already noted, workers are insiders. They are also heavily invested in the welfare of the organization. They have regular and intimate contact with the organization at every corner. And they are the ones who deliver the products and services. It obviously makes good business sense for leaders and for staff people who can influence the communication process to do so in the most conscientious and balanced way they can.

In the next chapter, we will delve more deeply into what I have called market-based strategic communication. It is our best hope for solving the serious information problem we otherwise will face if we do not do something.

Chapter Four

Market-Based Strategic Communication

Because there are surprises and remarkable events in life, we will never totally escape the need to communicate reactively. A certain amount of simple reporting of events will always go on inside organizations, but that should not be the exclusive or even the primary mode of communicating with employees. They need, as we saw in Chapter Two, connections between their work and the organization's strategy and goals; they need connections with customers if they are to do their jobs well; and they need connections with one another if they are going to weather the change and turmoil of the modern-day work organization.

Two Eye-Opening Events

Two events first opened my eyes to this reality when I was a communication manager at Xerox in 1978. First, in those days our publications and other communication programs were so highly regarded by our peers in other companies that they would often come to us to benchmark our practices (although then no one would have recognized the word benchmark as it is now used.) The experience would be very flattering and affirming, but then we would see the regular internal surveys of our employees and discover that *they* generally did not believe that communication at work was particularly good. The disconnection between what our employees (who obviously were the real customers for our efforts) thought and what outsiders thought was disturbing. We were succeeding outside but failing with our customers—our own employees. We needed to understand why.

The second event occurred at about the same time, when my new boss reviewed my proposed communication plan for the upcoming year. His blunt reaction was, "That's fine, but what's our communication strategy?" I was taken aback because I thought that I had just told him. It was a carefully developed plan with chapter and verse of proposed story ideas for our various publications and the new programs we as a company should be funding and launching in the near future for employees.

Didn't he get it, I wondered? I had proceeded to reiterate the major pieces of the plan when he stopped me cold. "No, no. Those are the *tactics* you want to use. I want to know what our strategy should be."

The two things eventually came together for me. Our employees were dissatisfied with the information they did or did not receive. My boss was asking about our strategy, and I was talking about the very tactics that had not been delivering a satisfactory product to our people. It was a moment of truth. Either we as a communication staff would continue with communication solutions that did not satisfy our customers' needs because those solutions were inevitably tactical, or we would finally develop a full-blown strategy to address their needs proactively. The truth is that the strategy did not come to us one day in a vision or even in one piece. We learned by trial and error and over long periods of weeks and months what we really needed to do.

This was all pre–total quality, and prior to the new awareness of customers and the need to listen to them. We had no road map for what we instinctively knew we had to do. So, we began by commissioning a communication survey of our audience. Such surveys were far from new at that time, but they had not generally been used as the basis for designing an entire communication strategy. Normal, day-to-day operational communication in organizations was mostly seen as something spontaneous that "just happened" among people and that could not be controlled or even influenced all that much.

Official communication, the other kind we thought we were responsible for helping to deliver, was what the leadership needed to *tell* workers. Ergo, how people felt about their operational communications was of interest but had little practical value because seemingly no one could do much about it. It was just another indicator of their current mood, their morale, and their satisfaction at work.

Armed with the survey results, we began slowly to answer some very important, if elementary, questions, the answers to which we had until then assumed we knew. Those assumptions had simply been reflected in our tactics:

- What information did Xerox employees *really* want and need at work?
- What were their preferred sources for that information?
- What were their actual sources?
- Aside from what we were doing with official information, what role should the leadership have been playing in managing the internal communication process?
- How about the management chain generally? What should they have been doing to improve communication?
- How about our CEO's personal efforts and those of his senior staff?
- Was there a role for the new technology that was just beginning to appear on the market? How could we use it cost-effectively?
- And finally, how could we hope to ever influence such a large process?

As we reflected on each question, we began slowly to understand the elements of the job that we had been neglecting because they seemed so much broader than our charter as a communication staff allowed. Many of the elements were on someone else's turf. What if the leadership or some of the staff guardians of secrecy told us that such things were not our concern? Was it not our job just to print what we were told and to make it as convincing as we could? What right did we have to meddle in what the leadership should say to employees? Did we have any of the clout we would need to get people to go along with the strategy?

A true strategy would have to be a carefully integrated collaboration among many staff groups. Could we persuade them to work with us and forget their turf concerns? How could we overcome their presumed tendency to close off the communication of difficult and sensitive issues? What could be done to break through the frozen middle of our organization where information tended to be blocked both on the way down and on the way up? And how could we persuade our leadership to support it all? Where would our allies be, and who were our potential adversaries?

These were indeed large questions for a group of people who heretofore had prided themselves on frank reporting of whatever news there was (even if the grapevine had been carrying the same stuff for several days in a much more down-to-earth style), and who largely saw their models in the public media. I wish I could say that we immediately implemented all we learned in a few brief months of research and reflection. But the truth is that it took a year or two to understand fully what was needed as the organization shuddered and stumbled through vast marketplace changes and eventually changed itself almost beyond recognition.

Making Communication a Strategic Process

Indeed, much of what had happened did not become crystal clear to me until a couple of years after I left Xerox, when I was a consultant and global competition was forcing my various corporate clients to think more carefully about how they could deliberately address the communication problems that were plaguing them.

I soon learned to distrust the tendency of the business press to tout the communication accomplishments of this or that high-flying organization. Their reports were more often hyperbole than reality. A memorable example was one of the nation's most respected high-tech companies, which engaged our consulting firm to help them assess their communication needs. They wanted us to do a study that would benchmark where they were now and give them cues for further action. The company is progressive and its culture is often held up as a model of what an enlightened organization ought to look like.

But in focus group after focus group, employees professed their ignorance of company strategy, company priorities, and even company results. They were bombarded with E-mail announcements, memos, videos, staff meetings, and leadership talk sessions, but none of this barrage of raw information had given them a clear context for what they were experiencing at work or for the issues that were shaping the organization's business strategy.

The subdivisions of the company had operated as vertical entities that carefully guarded their turf and their information. Little of this behavior was deliberate. It was simply a natural reaction to the traditional, hierarchical organization the founders had long ago created, and it had become standard operating procedure through the years. The result was employees who were poorly informed about major issues in their own company. I have seen the same phenomenon over and over again in my consulting work. Worst of all, I have seen it in companies I often read about in the business press as the best and brightest.

I now believe that every work organization needs to make its internal communication a management system. Any important process in the workplace is eventually systematized, that is, it is guided by a deliberate strategy. There is clear accountability for the behavior that is necessary to make the system strategy work, and there is training to make the accountability fair and enforceable. Strategy, accountability, and training are like a three-legged stool that supports any management system. Manufacturing fits the mold. Marketing fits the mold. Sales fits the mold. Indeed, almost any important work process eventually is reduced to a strategy, to accountability, and to training. Why not communication? My old boss was right when he asked, "What's the strategy?" He knew that strategy is the beginning of a successful system as opposed to something that happens according to whim, the needs of the moment, or personal style.

In an age in which information is increasingly recognized as a primary capital asset, we have been surprisingly cavalier about creating internal communication systems to match the organization's other key systems. Instead, we have tended to concentrate on media or technology in the mistaken belief that our primary problem has been timeliness and speed. Timeliness is undoubtedly important, but the more important issues are clarity and understanding. An unclear and poorly organized E-mail message delivered with the speed of light is still an unclear message. The challenge is to develop messages that further people's understanding, commitment, and productivity. That is hard work that requires clear thinking, careful planning and organization, and well-considered delivery. Small wonder that people would rather focus on the "gee whiz" aspects of media or technology than on the process of disciplined communication. The case of the high-tech company that had mastered the technique of delivering lots of message with little context is a perfect example of my point.

In the last dozen years, I have come to believe that the answer to this challenge is a strategic communication system that attempts to explain to the members of an organization what the marketplace and their customers are demanding of them, demands that they must meet if they are to stay in business and prosper. I use the marketplace as the first cause because that is where organizations must find the rationale for their actions and behavior.

A clear-thinking leadership is always preoccupied with what it has to do to meet the demands of the marketplace and its customers. That is the essential message of the total quality movement: listen intently to the customer, meet his or her requirements, and improve your processes continuously in response to the challenge of serving changing customer needs well.

Market-based strategic communication does the same thing. In the simplest terms, it is an effort to connect the organization's vision, mission, and business goals to the forces and opportunities that exist in the marketplace and that give purpose to the work that people perform. Its focus is on the business, on agreed-upon measures of success, and on the priorities that people must share to make the business succeed. It is also an effort to facilitate the efficient flow of clear, well-organized ideas and information among the members of a work organization, recognizing that such information is a vital resource for accomplishing their work. Its ultimate purpose is to provide a clear focus for the workforce so that its members can manage the work they do in order to achieve the goals of the organization.

The focused worker who sees clear connections between what he or she does and the success and accomplishments of the work organization is much more likely to be a satisfied and productive worker. What such workers have is what all of us seek in one form or another—a sense of purpose and meaning for the work activities that consume so much of their time and energy.

Workers who perform jobs with little sense of what those jobs mean to the organization are generally dissatisfied and frustrated, not to mention less productive than they would be if they knew the rules and results of the game they were playing. I often think that not giving people such information is like putting a team out on a field, not giving them the rules of the game, and withholding information about whether they are winning or losing. Such an approach is ludicrous in sports, but we often treat employees that way. To the extent that they do not see anything more than the particular tasks they perform, they feel like automatons who labor without meaning, except for pay and other tangible rewards. On the basis of my experience in talking with all kinds of workers in all kinds of organizations, I guarantee that their major negative issue is not feeling valued and appreciated for their contributions. The refrain is always the same: "They don't care about me. Why should I care (about them or about my work)?" It's not safe to voice such opinions openly, so they keep them to themselves and focus on the tasks at hand.

Why do people stay in organizations that treat them that way? Two answers always predominate: "The money is good" and "I like the people I work with." Satisfaction with the job and the company and the ability to make a worthwhile contribution—these things are seldom mentioned. The job becomes only a way to make a living and a social community in which the unappreciated toil together. That's not much of a recipe for a productive, quality-oriented workforce, if you ask me.

In the twenty-first century we will be operating in an organizational world in which people and information will be the critical assets. It is imperative that we learn how to lead people and manage information in such a way that both assets will be leveraged to the maximum. Productive and profitable companies have known that intuitively, but few have really understood fully how to carry on the process. Instead they have found their how-to models in the public media. Such an approach simply will not work in the new age in which we find ourselves. It is too divisive. It is too incomplete. It is too fragmented.

All-Purpose Revisited

To observe the contrast between reactive communication and market-based strategic communication, let's take a different look at the All-Purpose case. Let's see what might have happened if they had been communicating strategically and openly with their people all along. First, Gerard Power would have been carefully preparing the organization for the competitive challenges it was beginning to face. For months and years, he would have been talking about how the marketplace was changing and about how All-Purpose had to change in response to that marketplace. He would have been describing the market forces shaping the behavior of All-Purpose's customers, whether they were commercial or individual service users. He would have carefully linked All-Purpose's vision and mission to those market forces and would have been rationalizing the company's actions in reducing overhead as responses to those forces and their effect on the business.

For example, he might have chosen four key issues to talk about: the need to reduce costs, the need to increase worker productivity, the need to strike down the old notion of entitlement to a lifetime job, and the need for creative teamwork. For each of these issues, he would have woven a set of messages that illustrated clearly how they were linked to All-Purpose's measurable success and to the long-term common welfare of All-Purpose's people. Each of the issues would then have been reiterated by his senior staff in their discussions with their employees. The senior staff would have been knowledgeable and empowered to talk at any time to anyone about the impact of environmental issues on the business and what All-Purpose was doing to respond to those issues. They would have been equally knowledgeable about the competition and able to hold forth on who the competitors were and what they were capable of doing.

Likewise, All-Purpose supervisors at practically any level of the organization would have been informed through a variety of channels about the same general issues so that they could answer questions and argue the case for change intelligently. All of them would have known clearly that such communication was an expected and accountable behavior on which they would be evaluated in both routine research and in special upward evaluations by their employees. They would have understood that a primary part of their role was to listen and to act on innovative ideas and suggestions without the need for constant checking with their own supervisors.

The important outcome would have been a workforce that understood that it was for the first time in a competitive marketplace in which cost-effectiveness was an essential measure of performance. They would have known that quality service was expected and demanded and measured and that work processes were under continuous review. Their questions would have been respected and answered candidly, and there would be no doubt in their minds that their jobs were conditional and depended each year on company performance in the marketplace.

In all likelihood, they might not have liked some of the messages they were hearing about the need to control spending or about the fact that success was not a comfortable job with few demands and annual salary increases. They might well have resisted some changes and grumbled about the ones they did accept. But their final response would have been, "I don't like it, but I understand why it's necessary. They're doing the right thing."

Amazingly, the odds are that that response would probably have been the same one they would have given to the announced cutbacks. The reason? They would have understood that the cutbacks were the result of declining earnings that were threatening the company's competitive position in a tough marketplace, and they would have known the clear linkage between All-Purpose's competitive position and their jobs. They would not have seen the action as a mean-spirited response of an uncaring leadership.

No one would have cheered about the cutbacks, but when the local television reporter appeared at the power plant, he might well have gotten a reasoned response based on the facts from almost any employee he talked to. There would have been regret but much less bitterness. A large part of the reason would have been their trust and confidence that All-Power would do the best it could for its people in a difficult situation.

Are We Brainwashing?

One question inevitably suggests itself at this point: is strategic communication some sort of management brainwashing of the workforce? Some will argue that that is exactly what it is. Done with a heavy hand and with minimal regard for the truth, it would be the worst kind of propagandizing. But done as a sincere and balanced effort to educate people to the realities of the new marketplace and about how that marketplace influences and shapes company actions, it is an essential task today.

Strategic communication allows leaders to present a purposeful view of the organization, which everyone is free to accept or reject. If the logic is compelling and the messages true—two critical qualifiers for sure—the communication is both useful and reassuring, even when the news is bad, because what this kind of communication does more than anything else is make it clear to people that the leadership understands and is carrying out its responsibilities, anticipating problems and needs and acting on them. No less important, it presents a view of the world, a context—with all of its perils and complexities—in which the organization operates and acts.

Also, the new social contract, which makes the worker responsible for his or her own destiny, requires informed career decision making. Isn't it about time we gave people the honest information they need to make those decisions intelligently? If I am personally vulnerable in an organization in difficult circumstances, I certainly want to know what those circumstances are so that I can exercise whatever options I have.

Why Strategic Communication Works

I do not want to overstate the effects of good market-based strategic communications, but I have seen enough such cases to know that it works and that it can be a powerful way to unite people in support of a company position in difficult times as long as it is backed by consistent and supportive action—the well-known "walking the talk." Why it works is not really that hard to fathom.

For openers, it provides what I have been harping on here so far—namely, a context for people's work experience, a frame of reference, a compelling case for change that allows them to put events in their proper perspective. People are smart about work and their employment circumstances—smarter in fact than we have ever given them credit for. If you doubt that, lead a few focus groups of typical employees. My bet is that you will gain a renewed respect for their ability to cut through the nonsense and understand the realities of their situation.

Listen to the words of CEO Lawrence Bossidy of Allied Signal in a 1995 interview in *Harvard Business Review* ("The CEO as Coach," 1995) describing what he did when he took over the troubled supplier of aerospace systems, automotive parts, and chemical products. "In the first 60 days (of taking office) I spoke to probably 5000 employees. . . . I would stand on a loading dock and speak to people and answer their questions. . . . I knew intuitively that I needed support at the bottom right from the outset. Go to the people and tell them what's wrong. *And they knew. It's remarkable how many people know what's really going on in their company*" [italics added; p. 70).

Adding that he believed in "the burning platform theory of change," he says, "When the roustabouts are standing on the off-shore oil rig and the foreman yells, 'Jump into the water,' not only won't they jump, but they also won't feel too kindly toward the foreman. . . . They'll jump only when they see the flames shooting up from the platform. . . . The leader's job is to help everyone see that the platform is burning, whether the flames are apparent or not" (p. 70).

On the arbitrary use of authority, Bossidy says, "The day when you could yell and scream and beat people into good performance is over. Today you have to appeal to them by helping them see how they can get from here to there. . . . Do all those things, and they'll knock down the doors." He then adds, "You have to create clarity about the issues you're dealing with, and here I mean the business issues. . . . People have to know where they're going. What is victory? Where do you want to be? Every year, we set three goals that we put in front of people. It creates focus. . . . People need to be focused on what we're trying to do. We want them to believe that the goals we're talking about are real, that we can do it" (p. 72).

Proof of the effectiveness of Bossidy's views lies in company results. Three years after he took over, net income had risen from $359 million to $708 million. Operating margins had climbed during the same period from 4.4 percent to 8.5 percent, and the company's market value had climbed from $4.506 million to $9.8 million. Bear in mind that the period from 1991 to 1994 was largely one of slow growth in American business.

An equally interesting example of market-based strategic communication is a much smaller organization: Springfield ReManufacturing Corporation (SRC), formed in Springfield, Missouri, in the early 1980s from a money-losing plant of the old International Harvester Corporation. The plant remanufactured truck engines. At the time it was one of the most leveraged corporate buyouts in American business history. The new owners, who were the former plant management, began with $100,000 in cash and an $8.9 million loan. Jack Stack, the CEO of SRC when it came out of the strife-torn International Harvester of the Archie McCardell era, had long believed that people performed best when they were fully informed about the business. He had seen McCardell, as CEO, worsen old animosities between management and labor. His goal was to create a company of businesspeople in which everyone—from the janitor to the CEO—feels, thinks, and acts like owners.

The two pressing questions when Stack and his company began were How do we turn this thing that is failing into a viable business? and How do we do it quickly before we run out of money? Their vision was a no-nonsense statement, which nonetheless has great power: "We're trying to get through life." The goal was to turn a failing business around and survive. Their mission statement was equally to the point with two key statements: "Don't run out of cash. Don't destroy from within." In brief, keep the wallet from going flat, and don't do anything imprudent to hurt ourselves.

They decided that an important part of the answer to their problems was "open-book" leadership, a philosophy that required them to share information about the business openly and without reservation so that people could make informed decisions on the job. Each week, they assembled most of the workforce or their representatives and briefed them in what they called "the great huddle" on real-time results that workers could then immediately affect by their job actions and decisions. Their training process was focused primarily on business literacy—teaching people about how the business was run and what the key measures of success were.

They also agreed to share the wealth—or lack of it—in the form of monthly bonuses with the workforce, an element the SRC people insist is critical. The bonus measure is return on assets and charge-out rates, two concepts that all SRC people are intimately familiar with as a result of the huddles and the ongoing education of the workforce.

As one worker put it in describing why he felt like an owner, "They don't hide anything from us. There's no surprises. I know exactly what's happening with the company every week. I know where we're at financially." Says Stack in commenting on what he calls "The Great Game of Business," which SRC now teaches as a seminar on open-book management, "We work very hard at trying to create excitement. The whole aspect of our business is the aspect of our people. They make the changes, and they make the differences."

How well has SRC's version of market-based strategic communication worked? From a 1983 loss of $60,000, the company has grown to over $100 million in revenue; the number of employees has grown from 119 to more than 800; and the size of the company has grown from one operation to fifteen divisions in fifteen locations across North America. Most impressive of all, shareholder value has increased by 27,000 percent!

The beauty of market-based strategic communication is that it helps people make the all-important connection between their

efforts and the needs of customers. In the modern work organization, that connection has often been lost as people's work has
become more and more fragmented into singular tasks. One of the
great services of the total quality movement has been to restore this
connection. The craftsman of old gloried in the feedback of his customers as they admired his work and ordered more. This natural
human need to relate effort to outcome is strongly reinforced by
good market-based strategic communication.

As we have seen in the revised All-Purpose scenario, market-
based strategic communication also has the potential to take seemingly random and even painful events and focus more on their
significance than merely on the fact that they occurred. In short, it
explains events rather than merely retelling them. Done right, it
also portrays a world in which leaders are connected to reality. One
of the most damaging outcomes of reactive communication is to
portray leaders as victims, as whipped about by this surprise and
caught off guard by that event. It is not a comforting picture in a
world already full of uncertainty. Good strategic communication
demonstrates the leaders' grasp of the situation and their attempts to
formulate intelligent strategies. The winds of change may be pum-
meling us, but at least we know what direction they are coming
from and at what velocity and ferocity, so we can prepare.

Another great service of strategic communication is that it presents the all-important case for change. If we dislike change so
much, we need to understand why it is required. Changes have personal costs, and we need to believe that the costs are worth it. Otherwise, we will find ways to reject the changes that have been
called for.

Another contribution of strategic communication is that it
shows leadership actions as rational and considered. Now, of course,
if they are neither, all the communication in the world is not going
to change things. But if such actions are well-reasoned responses to
clear problems, the resulting connections can be very reassuring and
give people a sense that their leadership is on top of the game and

that their own work is meaningful in addressing the organization's needs. That's critically important because if people finally conclude that their work is meaningless, they lose interest and personal productivity. I would argue that the best workers are those who see meaning in what they do. That meaning allows them to transcend the day-to-day grind and small and large setbacks and to remain focused on their work.

A Strategic Communication Model

If what I say here is true, and I passionately believe that it is, where do you start in creating a strategic communication process? I would give the same answer that I inevitably give to my clients. Today's circumstances make the need for strategic communication far more relevant and necessary than it has ever been before. The best starting point is *research*. What I call the "organizational assessment" in my strategic communication model (the first part of which is shown in Figure 4.1) is the beginning of the research effort. Here the task is pretty straightforward.

A good organizational assessment process uses familiar tools to address the areas shown in the four boxes in Figure 4.1. First, if you want to know how the communication process is working right now in your organization, the logical way to find out is to ask the two key parties—the leadership and the employee audience—some pointed questions. First, to the leaders:

- What does the leadership need to communicate to the workforce?
- What is the essence of the business strategy? Why is it an appropriate strategy in addressing the market forces that are shaping company actions? What are those forces and how are they influencing customer behavior?
- What are the obstacles to success for the organization?
- What are the issues that most worry management as they contemplate the challenges they face in the marketplace?

Figure 4.1. Strategic Communication Model, Part 1.

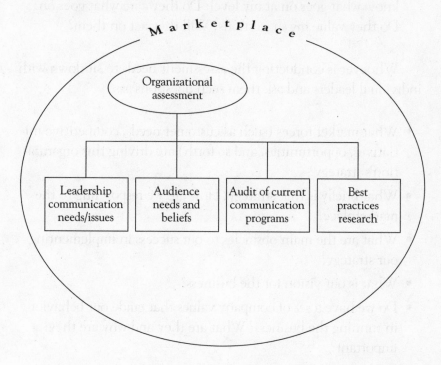

How do they propose to address those issues, and what does that mean for the organization's priorities?

These are but a few of the issues you need to understand if you are to design a suitable communication strategy to reach employees. Employees have their own questions:

- How are we doing?
- What are we trying to accomplish as a business?
- Why must we change past work practices? What urgency dictates such change?
- What are the priorities?
- What does it all mean at my level?
- What can I do to protect my job security?

- Can I trust these people? Do they care about me? Do they know what goes on at my level? Do they care what goes on? Do they value my suggestions? Will they act on them?

Whoever is conducting the assessment needs to sit down with individual leaders and ask them such questions as:

- What market forces (such as customer needs, competitive initiatives, opportunities, and so forth) are driving this organization's strategy?
- What briefly is that strategy? How are we responding to the marketplace?
- What are the main obstacles to our success in implementing our strategy?
- What is our vision for the business?
- Do we have a set of company values that guide our behavior in running the business? What are they and why are they important?
- In clear and simple terms what do you see as the critical success factors for the business? What do these factors say about what our priorities should be?
- What does success look like? What are the vital measures (market share, profitability, stock price, and so on) that tell us whether we are winning or losing?
- As you look out into the future, what worries you most? Where are the company's vulnerabilities?
- What do you want employees to understand better about the company and their jobs?

These and similar questions that are appropriate to the organization's particular circumstances begin to shape the nature of the leadership's communication task. They also yield a wealth of information and perspective about the business.

Employees need to be asked in focus groups questions like the following:

- Where do you now go to get information about the company and your job? Why there?
- Among all of those varied sources, which ones are the communication strengths (that is, the ones most useful to you, the ones you most trust?)
- Which ones are the communication weaknesses, that is, the least useful?
- Can you say what is missing from your communication experience? Why is it important to you?
- What is the impact of the various communication weaknesses on your ability to do your job? How do they handicap you?
- What suggestions or ideas do you have for action items that could address some of these needs?

Through such questions, you can begin to develop a very clear picture of people's communication experience at work. I have learned that employees are both wise and practical information sources for such questions. Typically, they want to understand the business and their customer and how they can better suit the customer's needs. They also want a clear signal that they count, that they are part of the process, and that someone is listening.

The activities in the other two boxes in Figure 4.1—audit of communication programs, and best practices research—are also important sources of information. What are your organization's current communication programs and how well are they functioning? Readership surveys, mini-questionnaires administered after communication meetings, informal discussions, full-blown written opinion surveys—all of these are essential tools in finding out what is or is not working in your present communications arsenal.

There are two sources for best practices. One is the body of standing communication research on employee information preferences at work, which is readily available from a variety of professional and commercial sources, and the other is the simple device of calling up companies known for their effective internal communication practices and interviewing them either by telephone or in person. In short order, you will usually have candid information on what techniques do or do not work for these companies. Because corporate culture is an undeniable influence on what works in a given organizational environment, your task is to pick and choose those practices that are most likely to succeed in your own organization.

There is nothing very mysterious in this whole assessment process, and it yields a wealth of information that can serve as the essential foundation for a strategy and for numerous action items.

Results of the Assessment Process

Figure 4.2 illustrates the steps resulting from the assessment process.

Visionaries and Missionaries. The second step in the strategic communication process is either the development of a vision and values statement or the examination of the present vision statement to see if it squares with the leadership aspirations and dreams that are uncovered in the interviews. For a long time I had trouble making a distinction between a vision and a mission. I finally arrived at a simple solution derived from the operational meaning of the two words.

Visions are the work of visionaries—a simple and not very profound truth. But who or what are visionaries? They are, quite simply, the people who look over the heads of the crowd and see things the rest of us somehow miss. Generally, they are able to express their vision in terms that engage the curiosity, the interest, and the imagination of the rest of us.

In recent years, work organizations have often trivialized visions, turning the most mundane kinds of statements about cus-

Figure 4.2. Strategic Communication Model, Part 2.

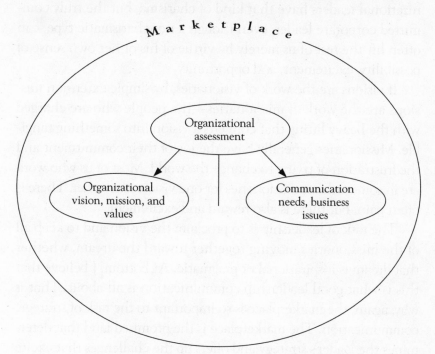

tomer service and quality into framed bromides to decorate conference room walls. Real visions can seldom be captured in a few simplistic words and phrases. They are more like dreams with an inspirational quality that people can connect with in a moment and decide they want to pursue. The truly effective leader often has the skill to arouse this kind of reaction in others by his or her clear passion for the vision. If that passion is missing, the vision probably is not truly a vision.

So, visions are crucial in providing the inspiration an organization needs when people become tired of their work or when they face discouragement. At such points the strong leader can once more hold out the vision and renew their energy. Think of Winston Churchill ("We will never give up"), Franklin Roosevelt ("The only thing we have to fear is fear itself "), and Martin Luther King

("I have a dream") and the picture becomes clear. Not many organizational leaders have that kind of charisma, but the truly committed corporate leader, even though a noncharismatic type, can often lift the rest of us merely by virtue of his or her own sense of possibility, excitement, and opportunity.

If visions are the work of visionaries, by simple extension missions are the work of missionaries—the people who are charged with the heavy lifting that converts a vision into something tangible. Missionaries generally have the joy of their commitment and the frustration of trying to change the world. Most of us who work are in some fashion missionaries for one vision or another. There is often pain, but there is also reward and excitement.

The task of leadership is to proclaim the vision and to keep all of the missionaries moving together toward the dream, whether that dream is inspirational or pragmatic. At bottom, I believe that this is what good leadership communication is all about. That is why, again, the marketplace is so important to the task of strategic communication. The marketplace is the promised land that determines the leader's strategy and offers up the challenges that excite the rest of us.

A third important element is the shared values by which the members of the organization will live. These values are critical because they identify the ground rules for their collective behavior. They signal what together they will cherish and despise as they work toward their vision. It is essential to announce these values and not to leave them to chance.

Jim Orr, the CEO of UNUM, says that he is absolutely convinced that people prefer to work for causes that are bigger than they are and to which they can willingly dedicate their energies and their talents. I believe he is right. Orr is an example of the kind of business visionary who inspires remarkable dedication and very clear focus because of his insistence that all company actions and initiatives must pass muster against the company's vision, mission and values. He leads with the goal of achieving measurable results as a product of group effort and group dedication from people who clearly understand and pursue a shared vision. The vision comes first; the results follow.

In interviewing UNUM employees in focus groups, I could find almost no evidence of the classic dissonance that exists in most organizations between what leaders say and do. Believe me, that is a remarkable finding, as anyone who has ever led a focus group will attest. The credit goes to Orr and his management team, who wrote the vision and insist on living by it.

Identifying the Issues to Be Communicated.   Two other products of the assessment shown in Figure 4.2 are summaries of the organization's communication needs and business issues. The list of communication needs is derived from the organizational assessment. For example, you might conclude from a series of management interviews that the company leadership desperately wants to

- Find ways to increase teamwork and break down turf boundaries in the organization
- Educate people about customer concerns and needs
- Show the impact on earnings of rising overhead costs
- Alert employees to the intentions and strategies of certain global competitors

At the same time, focus groups and/or surveys might reveal that employees

- Are frustrated that supervisors are not listening to their concerns or suggestions
- Question management's long-term commitment to quality and customer service
- Have little understanding of who the competition is and what kinds of threats they pose

- Believe that it is risky to express their candid views or to offer honest feedback when it is requested

- Complain that company leadership is invisible and out of touch

Such a list of needs obviously provides important clues for a respon-sive communication strategy, in terms of both content and action items.

If the vision is the soul of the strategy and the human informa-tion needs are its appetite, the organization's business issues and pri-orities comprise the heart of the strategy. They are the core of issues that the leadership must talk about repetitively if they are to get through to people. In most organizations there are typically five or six major business issues that are critical to success—things like the competition, the need to control costs, customer satisfaction, prod-uct and service quality, or issues peculiar to the business or indus-try. Each of these issues can be matched to one or more market forces that make it a critical success factor and then reduced to a core set of messages, as shown in Figure 4.3. For example, one of the key business issues for a particular organization might be: global competition forces us as an organization to look constantly for ways to make optimum use of all our resources.

In this example, the market forces that dictate that making optimum use of resources is a key issue for the company are global competition and the ability of low-cost producers to sell products at a cheaper price because of their labor-cost advantage in low-wage-rate labor markets. These forces exert undeniable pressure on the company and create the issue, which is a product of both how management perceives the market force and how it decides to respond.

By using global competition as the rationale for cost-effective management and the need to make maximum use of all company resources, the leadership can build a reasonable case for a variety of specific actions. Instead of random, ill-thought-out, and arbi-trary actions, these moves now appear to make some sense—

Figure 4.3. Matching Business Issues to Market Forces.

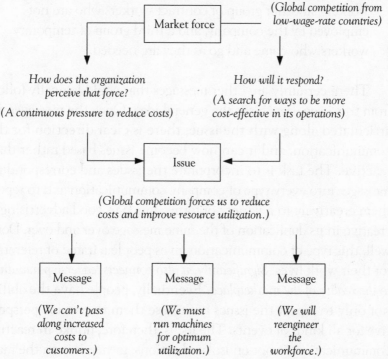

whether in fact as an affected employee you like or do not like their implications.

The key messages that might naturally be derived from this single issue could be as follows, depending on the market reality:

- In a global marketplace we do not have the flexibility to pass along our costs to our customers in increased prices. Therefore we must look for every opportunity to do things efficiently and to make maximum use of assets.

- One imperative way to maximize our assets is to put all production machinery, where possible, on a continuous run— seven days a week, twenty-four hours a day. We will need to schedule workdays to accommodate this necessity.

• The most efficient way to staff the business is to reengineer the workforce so that we employ a core group of full-time workers, another group of contract workers who are not employed by the company, and a third group of temporary workers who come and go as they are needed.

There certainly are other messages that could logically follow from this issue, but this is the general idea. Once the messages are articulated along with the issue, there is clear direction for the communication, and it can now become issues based rather than reactive. The task is to incorporate the issues and corresponding messages into every type of company communication and to repeat them creatively in a variety of forms, much as good advertising is creative in its duplication of the same message over and over. Done well, this type of communication gives people a frame of reference for their work lives. *Significantly, it also connects leadership initiatives to the reality of the marketplace.* Eventually, people have the ability not only to repeat the issues but to use them to provide perspective for all kinds of events. The focus, therefore, unlike in reactive communication, is not on isolated actions; rather, it is on the market forces that cause those actions and make them necessary and reasonable.

As an example, look at the message that it will be necessary to maximize resources by putting all machinery on a continuous run. I worked with the leadership of an automotive plant that faced this exact problem. The kicker was that employee work schedules needed to be arranged to accommodate this necessity. Anyone who has ever been around a manufacturing facility knows how sensitive an issue employee work schedules can be.

Working from the basic issue of global competition and the need to make maximum use of resources, it was relatively easy for plant management to show the connection between that issue and the action of instituting a continuous run in the factory. Understanding the potential disruption, the leadership opened discussions with the union leadership to persuade them of the necessity for this action and to win their support. They scheduled focus groups of bargaining-unit employees to listen to their concerns and to identify the kinds of schedules that would be least disruptive to their personal and family lives, and to explain the necessity for such a move. They also organized larger group meetings to explain further the necessity for the action and to answer questions and concerns.

The plant newsletter and employee meetings were used to explain the impact of lower third-world wage rates on the company's competitive position and to make the key point that an essential answer to such wage competition is greater automation and fully efficient use of plant assets. That such a move is far better than the alternative of exporting jobs to low-wage-rate countries was also emphasized. The meetings were also used as the occasion for making the point that the days of easy competition when each person had a particular job to which he or she could feel somehow entitled are gone. Further, it was pointed out that in this new world the task is for everyone to use his or her imagination in determining the most effective ways to accomplish the complex work tasks the company faces.

In this kind of market-based strategic communication, the primary messages are continually linked to the forces shaping company strategy. Traditional employee communication tends to focus on discrete actions which in and of themselves often make little sense to the workforce. Market-based communication is constantly educating employees about what the organization must do to serve its marketplace and succeed.

In the "good old days," in such a situation the new work schedule would probably have been announced without consultation or discussion and with the inevitable contract conflict between management and the union. The expectation would be that the workforce would simply deal with the new demands or, in the worst case, management would have to back off from a hardened position or accept the eventual need to move jobs elsewhere.

This brand of strategic communication obviously is more time consuming, requires more preparation, and is more demanding intellectually. But if we truly believe that human capital makes the competitive difference today, how can we argue with any legitimacy that there is no time for this kind of dialogue and logical explanation? Today's workers are intelligent people who need reasoned explanations and broad understandings if they are to be productive contributors.

Reducing Objectives to Tactics

Once the communication needs of both the leadership and the internal audience (and the external audience, for that matter) are clear, and once the business issues have been clearly identified and articulated, it is possible to begin to develop intelligent communication objectives for the organization.

If you were to look at the list of leadership and employee communication needs listed earlier, the following plausible communication objectives are a few that might follow for that particular organization:

- To encourage greater teamwork between and among work units and groups
- To expose employees to customer groups—their concerns, feedback, and expectations
- To report operating results fully and understandably
- To acquaint employees with competitors and their products and services
- To conduct more frequent town hall meetings in which employees could meet with and question senior management

There undoubtedly would be other objectives, but that is a sample of what might make sense as key objectives.

The problem in most work organizations is that people want to *begin* with the objectives without all of the preliminary reflection and analysis. That simply will not work because the objectives then turn out to be uninformed and, perhaps, simply wrong. In one sense, it would be analogous to a company introducing a product or service with virtually no market research, on the basis that they know only too well what the customer needs. Smart businesspeople just do not operate that way.

Once the objectives have been formulated, it is a rather simple matter to convert them into the right tactics. Figure 4.4 shows that this process is the part of the model that provides for the issues and messages, the programs that will be the best channels for delivering those messages, and the measures that will be established for

Figure 4.4. Strategic Communication Model, Part 3.

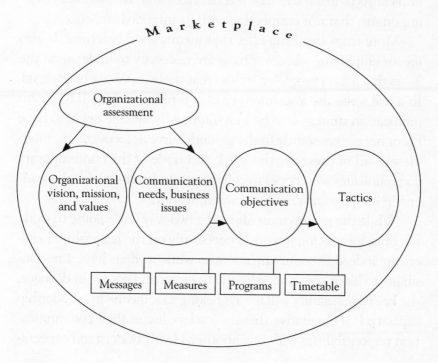

success, as well as an appropriate timetable. Let's look briefly at each of these things.

We have already talked about converting key business issues into messages. That process requires continuing review to be sure that both the issues and their respective messages continue to reflect the leadership's best thinking. For their part, company leaders should regularly spend time thinking carefully about what they want and need to say to the workforce, because those messages are terribly important in setting both priorities and tone.

Those who serve the communication process in an organization as staff consultants, writers, editors, and producers also need to be certain that they have a clear understanding of the issues and how they need to be presented. Obviously, that means that they must be in fairly close and frequent contact with the leadership if they are to do this part of their job correctly. They must also make it their business to monitor the content of the organization's communication efforts to make sure that it is balanced and complete and, more important, that it is connecting with its intended audience.

More than anything else, that means good listening. It also means employing whatever tools are necessary to understand the issues that are on people's minds so that those issues can be engaged. In a real sense the assessment process is never-ending. If the communication strategy is to be well informed, someone needs to have his or her ear constantly to the ground. Surveys, focus groups, interviews—all of these are the stock and trade of the contemporary communicator who hopes to collaborate and consult with the leadership in designing credible communications.

While the process must always be two-way if it is going to work, the onus for making it work is necessarily on the leadership. Leadership, indeed, is communication, so while workers have a responsibility to listen openmindedly and to report and engage in dialogue, the key responsibility will always belong to someone in a leadership capacity. It is imperative that the leaders discuss their communication responsibilities with one another, clearly understand expectations, and strategize their efforts jointly and collaboratively so that everyone is on the same page in executing the strategy.

Message Delivery

The communication programs that an organization puts in place are also important. Are they believable? Are they timely? Are they accessible? Are they what people want? All of these concerns call for some kind of measurement effort in the organization to answer those questions and to monitor the programs continuously.

In general, we know from the research data that most people prefer face-to-face communication when it is possible and if it is informative. They also like to meet in small groups with the boss so that they can get their questions answered and raise their concerns and complaints. Further, they like to see the leaders occasionally so they can size them up and ask them questions. That is particularly true when the organization is in some kind of trouble or going through massive change. Nothing works like face-to-face communication with the responsible leaders at such a time. All of this is well documented in the employee opinion research, and it needs to be part of the conventional wisdom of organizations.

The newest evidence is that people also like technology that they can access and manipulate at their convenience. E-mail, voice mail, faxes, and video conferencing are all appreciated for their immediacy, their flexibility, and their inclusiveness. What people do not like is that such technology can sometimes deluge them with more raw information than they can handle.

Providing for Continuous Improvement

The last step, presented in Figure 4.5, is to make the strategic communication process a continuously improving effort. That calls for some kind of evaluation and feedback from the intended audience and the use of that feedback to begin the organizational assessment

Figure 4.5. Strategic Communication Model, Part 4.

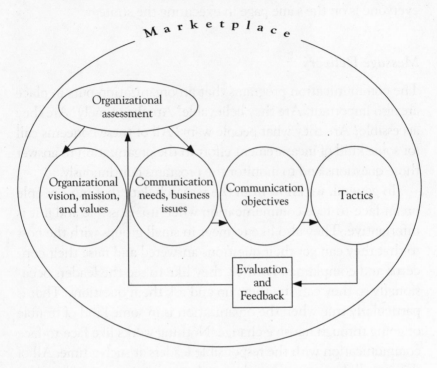

cycle all over again. In practical terms, that really means continuous monitoring to see if the communication is working and on target. We can look to advertising and marketing communication again for our model. No good advertising person would operate without continuing and persuasive research to determine the effect of the messages he or she is sending. That research may not be done with the precision and assurance of atomic physics, but it clearly indicates what is or is not working.

The final rendering of this strategic communication model in Figure 4.5 shows a communication process that is rational, flexible, informative, and responsive to the needs of all members of the organization. It also recognizes the right and need of employees to understand the environment they work in, both the larger marketplace and the smaller—though to the participants often more real—workplace.

My intent in creating this model is to show how organizational leadership can make the critical connection between the workplace and the marketplace in which the organization must make its mark. I have outlined the process in the hope that others can tailor it to their own reality. This market-based communication model addresses an organization's big issues and big picture. In that sense, it is a macrocommunication process, and it is vitally important if people are to understand the big issues that govern an organization's behavior.

Let's look next at microcommunication, the process by which most communication between a work supervisor and his or her employees actually takes place. It is the interaction of the two types of communication—macro and micro—that ultimately determines the quality of the communication process in any given organization. The challenge is to see how this second communication process can be better aligned with the organization's larger issues.

Chapter Five

Aligning Individual Effort with Organizational Goals

Between 1981 and 1991, 29 million American workers lost their jobs. That is roughly equivalent to the combined populations of New York City, Los Angeles, and Chicago. It also represents approximately one in three of the more than 100 million people employed in the United States in the baseline year of 1981. However you measure it, it is a staggering number.

Many would argue that it could not be helped. They would point to the wage pressures that forced American companies to begin a slimming-down process, to make themselves, in the favorite phrase from the corporate lexicon, "leaner and meaner." They would point to the major shift in the American economy from manufacturing to service. They would argue that in that same period many people simply moved from higher-paid manufacturing jobs to lower-paid service work, but that the good news was that they still found employment. They would point out correctly that in 1991 almost 117 million people in this country were still employed—a growth of 17 million jobs in the ten-year period in question. They would claim that whatever the losses, we were still one of the strongest economies in the world. And they would be right.

But what they would be likely to gloss over in their explanations is the human cost of this shift: the lost income as people moved from higher-paid manufacturing work to various service jobs, and the residue of fear and bitterness that has come with this change. Much of this lingering sense of betrayal among American

workers stems from their view that they are entitled to a job practically as a birthright.

The Changing Nature of Work

In his book *Job Shift* (1994), William Bridges makes the crucial
point that today's organization is rapidly being transformed from a
structure built out of jobs into what he calls "a field of work need-
ing to be done." What have traditionally been called "jobs" he refers
to as "artificial units" and "patches of responsibility." He also asserts
that when the work that needs to be done changes constantly, we
cannot afford the mentality that sees jobs as boxes on an organization chart that are somehow "owned" by jobholders with regular
duties, hours, and salaries.

Jobs are artifacts, he says, of the days of factories, mass production, and repetitive tasks. They also reflect the bureaucratic mentality that once enabled us to organize work and apportion so many
layers of managers to oversee so many jobs to make sure that they
were done satisfactorily (Bridges, 1994).

Today's workplace model is more like the family farm of an earlier agricultural society on which there were peaks and valleys of
work and a large pool of labor to do that work. The answer in that
society to the question of how to organize that labor was the family unit augmented by one or more hired hands who were brought
in to help at peak periods and who did whatever needed to be done
at the time. The hired hand was not a specialized worker; instead,
he moved from task to task to accomplish the work of the day, and
he did so with limited supervision.

Understanding Human Needs on the Job

Some experts claim that the new workforce will be composed of
roughly one-third full-timers, one-third contract people to whom
the employer will make limited commitments about employment

longevity and rewards, and one-third temporary workers who will come and go as needed, much like the farmhand of our old agricultural economy.

Whatever the actual proportions turn out to be, the communication implications are tremendous. How is such a workforce to be motivated? How are they to be kept focused? Is there any possibility of employee loyalty under such circumstances? To say that it will be a challenge is a serious understatement.

Historically, managers have been able to supervise people mostly by watching them. Were they working at the appropriate pace? Was the quality of their output satisfactory? Did they produce sufficient quantity? What about their attitudes? Were they cooperative? Disruptive? Flexible? Those were all things that the supervisor looked for and rewarded and punished as appropriate.

Today we know that that system will not work. Demanding customers want workers who are empowered to address their needs on the spot. They do not want to stay on hold on the telephone while someone gets permission for a simple, commonsense action to address a routine problem. And if they do not get quality products and services, they will simply choose another supplier. So, new ways clearly must be found to lead and communicate with today's workers. The questions are: What are those new ways? and How do we learn how to communicate in the new work organization?

The answer, like the answer to so many problems, lies in understanding human needs on the job. If we take away job security as a given, think about what people most need in the workplace. The list is fairly clear: They want to know what's expected of them. They want to know how well they are meeting expectations. They want to believe that both they and what they do are important. They want to identify with a meaningful cause larger than themselves. And they want to know how they can best contribute, how they can involve themselves in the tasks to be done.

One way to understand how to deal with the communication needs of the worker in the twenty-first-century organization is to construct a model that portrays normal human needs on the job. If we accept Bridges's view that the traditional notion of a set and secure job is becoming obsolete, how do we accommodate that rev-olutionary change in the model? In my view, the final version turns out to be not a whole lot different from what it always needed to be but in truth seldom was in our traditional, paternalistic, and hier-archical work organizations.

The First Question

I would argue that the most basic of job communication needs has always been to provide direction to the worker. Even in a nontra-ditional, fast-paced information-age organization, people need to understand what is expected of them. They certainly have to be prepared to exercise initiative and good judgment and to accept what is called empowerment; but someone first has to help them understand what the day-to-day responsibilities are if empowerment is truly to mean anything.

Given that the traditional nature of "a job" is changing, how can those who supervise work help people understand what their new job is? Think back to your very first job or even your most recent job change. In all likelihood what bothered you most was the question of whether you would succeed or fail. A first job is a combination of high excitement and high fear. Can I do it, whatever it is? Will I measure up? Will I finally meet my Waterloo at work?

I remember clearly my first job out of graduate school as a very young high school teacher. I recall getting up on the first few morn-ings with slight feelings of nausea at the prospect of facing dozens of challenging adolescents. Not that I did not want to be there; it was a matter of wondering if I could control things, keep the stu-dents engaged and interested, and create the classroom experience I anxiously wanted to provide.

Three years later, when I gave up the teaching career I could no longer afford as a young family man to enter corporate life, my question was, Can I really make it in business? Will this work? Or years after that, when I started consulting, I asked myself, Am I a fraud? Would the consultant police of my fears find me and arrest me for giving out bad advice? Or impersonating an expert? To answer any of these questions, I first had to know: what is my job?

For me, such questions about human needs at work have come together to form a continuous, circular model that begins to describe the normal day-to-day communication that should (but often does not) take place in any workplace. I have chosen a circle because I think the process is never-ending. In an effective organization the worker is always learning and moving from one comfort and experience level to another. Figure 5.1 shows the first piece of the model: What is my job? Where are the boundary lines? Where do I have flexibility and in what areas of my work am I expected to exercise initiative and discretion? I need my supervisor, group leader, or team facilitator to help me understand what I need to do to earn my keep and to be regarded as a real contributor.

It makes no difference if I work in a new-age company in which I am likely to be employed only as a temporary worker or if I work in a company in which I can look forward to years of uninterrupted employment—the question is the same: What do you expect of me? One of the first communication tasks of any

Figure 5.1. The Manager's Communication Role, Question 1.

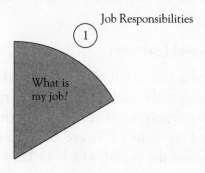

Job Responsibilities

supervisor is to address that question on a continuing basis. With-out that information, we look to the left and to the right and begin to invent work to fill our days.

In the new-age company the question is more compelling, if not baffling. If there is what Bridges calls a field of work, then show me my place in the field and tell me what you are up to and why, so I can manage my time with you most productively. Presumably, I would not be here if I did not have the skills to contribute, so help me to understand how I can add value by my presence.

The practical behavior required of the supervisor in this sit-uation is pretty straightforward and can be roughly summarized as follows:

- Provide clear descriptions of people's responsibilities and roles; talk about expectations.
- Set agreed-upon priorities and deadlines.
- Supply the information needed to do the job.
- Where possible, involve employees in planning, decision-making and implementing changes.
- Link employees' job responsibilities to organization strategy and priorities.

It's pretty much Supervision 101, but it's critically important to the person being supervised, because it begins to define the work, the working relationship, and expectations.

The Second Question

A second question follows hard on the heels of the first one if we are looking at the problem from the perspective of the employee. It is, very simply: How am I doing? Am I measuring up to your needs and expectations? Figure 5.2 illustrates this second, all impor-tant piece of the puzzle, which we know by the familiar name of

Figure 5.2. The Manager's Communication Role, Question 2.

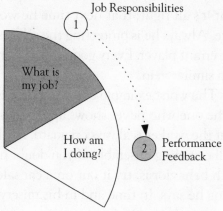

Job Responsibilities

What is
my job?

How am
I doing?

Performance
Feedback

"performance feedback." The employee states, Provide me with some measure of my performance so that I can make adjustments.

A key part of the quality process is measurement. The quality gurus know full well that people cannot improve their performance at any task unless they have a measure of their success or failure. Further, they need to have that measure quickly available so that they can make continuous adjustments. A critical role of the supervisor is to involve himself or herself in this measurement process and to become a coach and a teacher. In the best organizations, this is a key communication role of anyone who would supervise other people.

In the unenlightened organization, that role is usually perverted to that of, primarily, judge and evaluator. Hence, the performance appraisal, rather than being merely a confirmation of lots of small discussions during the year, now becomes a deadly serious report card and a means of doling out salary adjustments.

Good supervisors are almost always good coaches who know how to correct performance positively. One of my personal favorites is football coach Lou Holtz. If a player has just made a serious mistake, Holtz will take him out of the game and give him immediate feedback on what he did wrong. But in seconds he has an arm around the player's shoulder, comforting him and reassuring him that it's all right; that next time he won't make that kind of mistake. Always he is protecting the self-respect and personal worth of the errant player. Every good supervisor should learn how to coach in a similar vein.

The worst example of a supervisor is the low reactor. He or she is the one who never shows approval or disapproval. The result is that the worker is always on guard, not knowing if he is performing well or failing miserably. If you doubt how powerfully disorienting such behavior is, try it out on a car salesperson. Do not react to a thing he says. In time and in his misery, he will almost be ready to give you the car just to get a rise out of you. Ask any salesperson which customer he or she dislikes most. My money is on the low reactor.

Supervisors or team leaders who are low reactors always leave their people guessing. For some of them, I suspect this is a deliberate strategy, a kind of parental withholding of reaction. For others, I believe it is a result of their beliefs about human nature. Whatever the cause, it is no way to lead a workforce. Some misguided managers use this behavior as a manipulative technique to keep people off guard or on their toes—their position being that if you let people know they are doing a good job, they will relax and stop performing as well. This position is perhaps best summed up by the senior manager I once heard say, "If you tell them they're doing well, they stop trying. If you tell them they're doing badly, they lose hope. Better not to tell them anything."

Unfortunately, too many people share this strange view of human motivation in the workplace. It would be like going to a football game and not cheering for your team as they move the ball down the field for fear they will stop trying. Suffice it to say that the effective manager lets people know how he or she views their performance in honest and helpful terms.

Once again, the supervisor's expected behavior in response to this question is pretty traditional stuff, which probably should not be surprising. One of today's traps is to believe that change is forcing totally different and unique kinds of behavior. I doubt that. What makes organizations go is human relationships, and the elements of good relationship-building do not change, because humans are humans irrespective of new organizational structures or new information technology, which—whatever else they can do—cannot replace a warm handshake, a smile, a pat on the back, or a comforting voice. So, here is the list of behaviors for responding to "How am I doing?"

- Provide feedback—positive and negative—on performance.
- Tell employees what they have done right as well as what they have done wrong.
- Discuss mutual actions for performance improvement.
- Make feedback a frequent and timely activity.
- Learn how to listen effectively and how to coach people so they can improve their performance.

The older I get, the more I wonder if the process of performance feedback should ever be anything but developmental. The practice of tying it to merit increases strikes me as a bankrupt practice. I have rarely met anyone who really believes that organizations reward performance equitably with money. Pay for performance is the fantasy of human resource managers much more than it is a belief of typical workers. But I have also never met anyone who did not want to know in some fashion if he or she was doing the job satisfactorily.

The Third Question

When people know what is expected of them and that they are performing at a competent level, another very powerful communication need begins to make itself felt. Let's assume that someone has been on the job for a year or two, feels very comfortable with his or her responsibilities, typically works well over forty hours a week willingly, and will go the extra mile when it is called for. What does that person now need?

The answer to that question is found in the answer to the question shown in Figure 5.3, which is, simply: Does anyone care? I come in here every day, give it my best and make personal sacrifices for the good of the organization. Does anyone notice or appreciate my work?

As a consultant I have always been struck by how rarely this natural human need is satisfied at work for most people. The one complaint I have consistently heard from the employees I have interviewed is the lack of recognition and appreciation they experience for their work. In the new-age organization the odds are that

Figure 5.3. The Manager's Communication Role, Question 3.

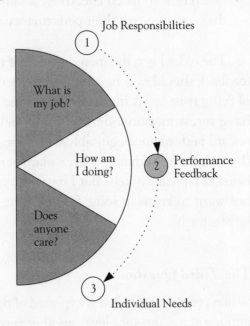

this situation will worsen rather than improve. If workers pass through an organization either on a temporary basis or at least with a sense of a conditional relationship to the organization, it is unlikely that they will feel particularly appreciated. Even if they are as permanently employed as economic results permit, there is a good chance that they will be worked hard to keep up with customer demands on a lean workforce. That is not a particularly good formula for feeling appreciated at work.

So what is the answer?

A now-deceased Jesuit priest with whom I occasionally led workshops on changing worker needs said it better than I ever could. His name was Tom McGrath, and he was a professor at Fairfield University, a small Jesuit college in Fairfield, Connecticut. His ability to connect with no-nonsense business leaders was amazing. He was a short, white-haired man with the demeanor of a second-generation Boston Irishman, which he was. He had a keen intellect edged with a quick and bright sense of humor. He had been traditionally educated in the church and had evidently reflected long on the meaning of that education and of his own vocation.

He was fond of reminding people in our workshops of the traditional ways in which people have been led in organizations. There were three traditional values, he would argue—authority, loyalty, and discipline—that were the truly vital values that made organizations work. Using stories from his family background and his experience as a priest, he would first make the point that authority was typically backed by some form of "the club." In other words, if you don't do what I say, I'll punish you because I have the right to. His invariable line at this point was to quote Paddy the Irish cop saying in his brogue as he raised his night stick, "It's not that I hates you that I beats you. It's because I have the authority to do so."

Then he would argue that leaders cannot manage by authority anymore because if they try to, people will rebel and, in some fashion, get even. He would cite examples from the rebellious child to the terrorist bombing civilian targets in revenge for real or imagined hurts to illustrate that that method is not going to work in the modern age.

The second traditional value, he would say, is loyalty. Then he would point out that loyalty in his experience meant blind loyalty. My family—right or wrong. My church—right or wrong. My country—right or wrong. Quickly he would add, "But this won't work with educated, sophisticated people, who want to know why they should be loyal, who want reasons." So, to request blind loyalty is a fool's approach.

The third traditional management value, he would say, is discipline. Typically that meant discipline administered by someone who thought that by virtue of his position it was his right to do so. The person being disciplined was supposed to accept that discipline uncomplainingly, but, he would add, people will no longer do that in the modern age if they think the discipline is unfair.

He would remind the audience of hard-nosed corporate types that if they insisted on leading by virtue of authority, loyalty, and discipline, "They will get you." They will be unproductive. They will ignore quality. They will insult your customers. They will do little more than go through the motions. They will get you.

And if that didn't register, Tom McGrath would take them all back to their family relationships—with spouses, with children—and he would demonstrate that even there, they could not lead by authority, loyalty, and discipline. You could see the consternation on their faces as they reflected with a mixture of agreement, frustration, and anger on the truth of what he was saying. He would sympathize with them from his experience in an autocratic, hierarchical church, insisting all the time that they had no choice. He would allude briefly to the ways his own church was changing. He would tell them that they had to face the changes and somehow change their leadership style. All of this happened in the 1970s and early 1980s, just as the impact of today's powerful organizational shifts was beginning to be felt.

Then Tom McGrath would offer his new paradigm, which was all the more remarkable because it was really a restatement of Gospel values. He would tell his skeptical audience that the answer was to manage through *love process*. You could immediately see the reservations written large on the faces of his audience as he uttered the phrase "love process," but they sat in rapt attention waiting for him to tell them what he could possibly mean by such a statement. And then he would begin to explain what he meant in clear and compelling terms.

Comparing love process to the relationships they all knew in their personal lives, he would draw the appropriate parallels. First, he would say, if you love me, you cannot lie to me. Without honesty, we have no relationship. And he would relate a personal story to illustrate the damage a lie does in a trusting relationship.

Second, he would make the point that people who love one another say so. Without that declaration of caring, it is difficult to maintain the relationship. So, he would tell them that they had to find good things to say to people, and he would tell a story of parents who brought their young boy to him for counseling. When he asked them if they ever complimented him, they said that there was little they could find to say in a positive vein. His response was, "How about the ceiling in his room? Is it clean?" When they acknowledged that, yes, his ceiling was clean, he would say, "Fine. Then tell him he runs a great ceiling."

Only half facetiously would he make his point that you can find something positive to say about everyone. He knew full well that his listeners could find plenty of negatives to offer their employees but that those negatives did nothing to promote a working relationship.

The third part of love process, he would say, was touching. Here you could sense quickly that he was skating on thin ice in the politically correct environment then starting to take shape. Lovers touch in beautiful, exquisite physical ways he would say, and then he would quickly add, "But that's not what I'm talking about. What I mean is *appropriate* love touches between two people who care about each other." He would ask them to find the appropriate love touches to use with their people, much as he, the celibate priest, did with the college students he taught.

He would tell the story of his Fridays at Fairfield when the Jesuits held their weekly cocktail party at the close of the day—black-suited figures moving purposefully to their campus rendezvous. He would be locking his door with anticipation to head up the hill to join his friends for a well-earned scotch when a distraught student would appear as he turned the key. "Father, I've got to talk." He would unlock the door and sit down and listen for the next hour or more. "He knows, and I know," he would say, "that it's a beautiful love touch as he unburdens himself, and I listen. . . . The two most beautiful love words in the English language are uh-huh."

The last sign of love process that Tom McGrath would offer the audience he now held in the palm of his hand was what he called "undoing." Telling them that they were bound to screw up sometimes, he would say that they needed to be able to say they were sorry when they had gotten it wrong. Rhetorically, he would then ask, "Have you ever heard a boss say she was sorry? Have you ever heard a politician say he was sorry? Have you ever heard a priest say he was sorry? It's sick! When we screw up, we have to have the courage to say, I'm sorry."

Then he would bring them back to his original point about authority, loyalty, and discipline and remind them that you cannot run an organization without those values. It was now clear that he meant authority based on respect, loyalty based on caring, and discipline that came from within rather than being administered externally. Love process was the difference in leading people effectively.

I watched dozens of such audiences through the years and in every case I saw them move from their initial skepticism about what this aging priest could possibly teach them about managing people to a warm acceptance of his wisdom. The vision he was drawing for them was of the servant-leader, the person who leads from his or her caring.

I believe that in today's organization the servant-leader is the only kind who can succeed in the face of change and in the fading days of entitlement. Look at the best-run companies with their emphasis on honesty, human dignity, and teamwork and decide for yourself what works or does not work in the new organization—whether that organization is a mature company in a low-growth business or a fast-growing, ad hoc kind of organization. I believe that the behaviors that work in leading people are essentially the same for both organizations.

What are the operational elements of the answer to the question, Does anyone care?

- Take time to listen and talk honestly with employees; value them as people.
- Practice management by wandering around.
- Hold staff meetings in which people have the opportunity to express their ideas and concerns.
- Solicit feedback about your own leadership style.
- Recognize and act on people's ideas.
- Practice common day-to-day courtesies and civilities.

As a psychologist, Tom McGrath always acknowledged the difficulty of managing in this fashion. An inevitable part of his message was to warn his listeners about the dangers of stress and how it could wipe out their best intentions and their concentration. He would advise diversion—exercise, travel, music, anything to renew their ability to handle the inevitable stress from managing in this way.

The Fourth Question

I would maintain, on the basis of my own experience, that if people get satisfactory answers at work to the first three questions—

What's my job? How am I doing? and Does anyone care?—they begin to feel a part of something larger than their own set of interests. It is at this point that they begin to use the pronoun "we" in connection with their work. We believe this. We do things in such and such a way around here. We accomplished such and such. The transition from "I" to "We" is a critical moment at work, and it signifies that the individual has begun to feel part of something bigger than himself or herself.

It is the supervisor's or manager's job to promote that identification, first by addressing the first three questions, then by responding to the two questions that follow. The first question that people typically ask when they reach this point is: How are *we* doing? This question is the next piece of the manager's communication model (see Figure 5.4). The question is based on the normal human need

Figure 5.4. The Manager's Communication Role, Question 4.

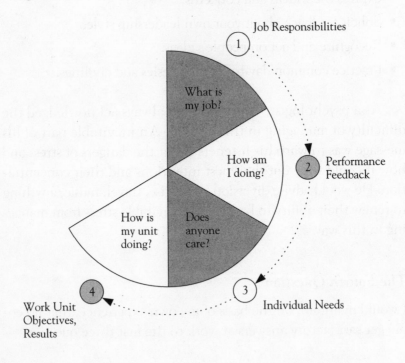

to want to identify with a team effort and to understand how the team is performing.

Once again, the behaviors that respond well to this question are pretty routine stuff:

- Share general business information on a timely basis.
- Discuss work group objectives and how they match overall organizational objectives.
- Recognize work group accomplishments.
- Discuss the need for work group performance improvement.
- Find opportunities to assemble the group for dialogue or celebration.

In general, do whatever it takes to foster a sense of a working team.

The Fifth Question

The logical flow of the model is from individual need to integration into a group. So, the next step is to raise the level of abstraction and give people the opportunity to identify with a larger reality. It is such a clear human need. Look at people on the streets wearing college sweatshirts, professional team jackets and hats, and even company logos on all sorts of clothing and possessions. We need to proclaim that we are somebody because we belong to something worthwhile.

So, the next question in the model, illustrated in Figure 5.5, is: Where are we headed? What are our vision, mission, and values? As we saw in Chapter Four, that is a powerful question. Supervisors and other managers who can proclaim a vision and a mission in convincing terms are our finest motivators in the organization. We should try harder to get them to fulfill that role because they are so credible with their people. In the same light, work supervisors need

Figure 5.5. The Manager's Communication Role, Question 5.

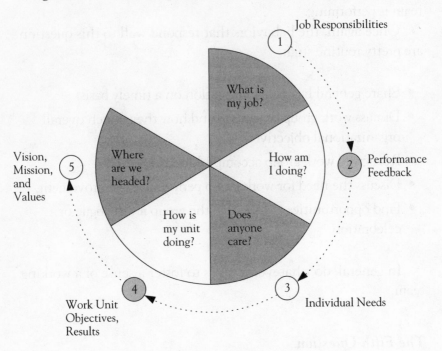

to know and internalize the value system of the organization because it defines the rules which they and their work group will all play by in this particular game.

As entitlement fades as an organizational expectation, it will be critical to provide something to take its place. George Fisher, former CEO of Motorola and now CEO of Eastman Kodak, understands this basic fact. As he works to change Kodak from a paternalistic organization with high levels of job entitlement to a lively, innovative competitor, he keeps reminding people of the need to respect the dignity of individuals and to appeal to their pride as they reengineer that great organization for its twenty-first-century destiny. Dignity, self-respect, and pride are important company values that he wants to foster in place of the old automatics of job security, regular raises, and unearned bonuses. Some may not like the trade he offers, but such values can help people through this kind of significant change.

In practice, this question requires the supervisor to

* Gain a personal appreciation and knowledge of the organization's vision, mission, and strategic direction.
* Internalize the company's value system and behave accordingly.
* Show personal conviction and commitment to the vision, mission, and strategy.
* Relate work group experience to the vision, mission, and values and help keep people focused.
* Be present to the workforce in ways that make them feel they are being led by someone who understands and cares.

The Sixth Question

Where large doses of this kind of leadership are commonplace, you will inevitably hear people ask the most important question they can in any organization: How can *I* help? Interestingly, that question (illustrated in Figure 5.6 as the final piece of the model) is a gift that the worker can either give freely or withhold begrudgingly. It is a response to high-quality leadership. It cannot be forced from someone against their will. It cannot be cajoled or threatened out of anybody. It can only be offered by someone who is willing to offer it.

More significantly, I would argue that it is the *beginning* of commitment, of empowerment, and even of individual productivity. Particularly in recent years, I have seen numerous organizations say, in effect, that beginning on July 1, we will be a quality-oriented, customer service company; or as of January 15, we will empower all of our employees to make decisions. They are not quite that blatant, but almost. It is as though they believe that a mere proclamation will make it so.

The truth is that individual commitment to organizational goals

Figure 5.6. The Manager's Communication Role, Question 6.

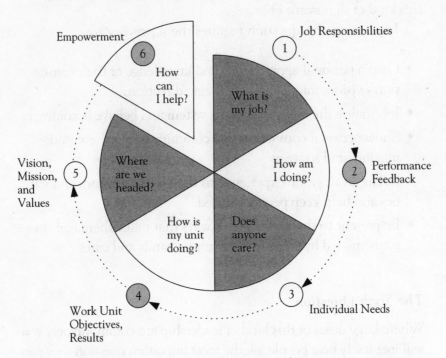

is what makes these things real, and the key person in unlocking the talent and gifts of individual employees is a supervisor or other leader who cares and knows how to lead people through effective relationship building and maintenance. Again, in operational terms the behavior that is required to make that happen is not particularly mysterious. What is required to nurture the employee who wants to commit his or her talents is a boss who

- Provides genuine opportunities for involvement.
- Empowers people to take the initiative and make decisions without second guessing them.
- Supports the risk takers even when they make a mistake.
- Recognizes and rewards true contribution.

- Encourages and supports cross-functional collaboration.
- Promotes mutual trust.

Establishing Accountability

The important question is: how do we create this paragon of a leader? I think the answer lies first in careful selection and then mainly in accountability for the desired behavior. Once we make it perfectly clear that this is our vision of the twenty-first-century work leader, as long as we seek out and appoint those people to the positions and inspect and reward this kind of behavior, it will happen. We got bosses in so many of our organizations because we made it clear that that is what we wanted—people who could be tough enough to accept and use authority, who demanded loyalty to themselves, and who were not afraid to punish what they saw as transgressions. If that is no longer what we want, we had better make it clear that that kind of behavior will not be rewarded or even looked at kindly.

It is hard to prove or disprove, but my own experience and observation tell me that much of what passes for leadership even today, in the twilight of the twentieth century, is still heavily tinged with the old-time management style. It is not hard to understand why: our models have typically been from that old mold. Even respected business publications still tend to glorify the blood-and-guts managers who make unpopular decisions. To be sure, that emphasis is changing as enlightened people read the changing times and understand that the challenges of a global economy require us to see human capital as the most precious asset we have in organizations. But the change is slow and uneven, and certainly it has always been less demanding to be a boss than to be a caring leader.

The other obstacle typically raised by managers and supervisors is the claim that they do not have time to manage people this way. I recall being part of a study team at one company trying to find out why its field managers were not communicating more effectively with their people. One day, a sales manager I was interviewing in a branch office interrupted the conversation and took out a notepad and began writing a long list of activities for which he was responsible. He turned the pad toward me and said, "Look, this is what I get paid for. Where do you see communication on this list?"

I saw no sign of the word and admitted it to him. He then added, "I'm as good as my last thirty days worth of sales results. But I'm a smart guy, and I know that if you take time to communicate with people you get results. So I promise you: if I ever get the time, I'll start managing people this way."

It was a primary learning experience for me. What I finally understood was that we will never address this issue as long as we see it as an add-on to all of the other things we do when everything else is done, a kind of extracurricular activity. Instead, we need to understand effective supervisory communication as a means to an end, as a way to enable the work process rather than as an activity that we perform if we have the time and if it matches our style. The real solution is to make it an accountable part of every manager's job.

I am often asked by clients how to enforce this kind of accountability. It is a good question. The answer, after the right kind of people have been selected, is to define and describe the kind of leadership and the kind of communication we must have in our organizations. That means articulating a set of shared values that make it clear how we will function. It also means telling people in leadership positions that they will be held accountable for this kind of behavior. And it means providing the educational and training resources to make the accountability fair.

One more thing it means is that some kind of measurement device is needed to make sure it is happening. The best device I know of is employee opinion surveys, which allow employees to comment on the leadership skills of their immediate managers. Some organizations now routinely use such surveys to determine who is or is not leading and communicating effectively. In the best cases, these surveys are used for developmental purposes, and managers are steered to training and counseling opportunities. If they do not show the proper improvement, they are moved to other positions in the organization that take them out of the role of leading people. Not everyone is suited to a leadership role. Indeed, it may be that few people have this kind of talent and patience.

The Payoff

The skeptics may well ask if this kind of change in the traditional role of the manager is worth the effort. Some object, saying that it will mean chaos in the workplace as we all learn to manage through some variation of Father McGrath's love process. I would respond that Father McGrath was a Jesuit pragmatist of the first order. He abhorred chaos and came to believe after long reflection that the only way to restore authority, loyalty, and discipline to their rightful place as organizational values was to give them a new and different foundation better suited to the modern world. He was no patsy.

Happily, some people in leadership roles in organizations are natural communicators. It is in their genes perhaps; certainly, it must be somewhere in their nuturing. They see the value of managing by human presence, and they go comfortably to where the workers are and speak to them in terms that mean something to the workers. One such manager at a coal mine in Southern Illinois expressed his opinion about communicating with his crew with as powerful a statement as I have ever heard on the subject. He said to me one day over lunch, "You've got to believe in this stuff like you believe in God to make it work. If you don't believe in it," he went on, "you'll lose your patience and your will and give up and just be a boss. Honesty and straight answers are the key, but you have to have the fortitude to hang in when people ask the same questions over and over—maybe to test the consistency of your views or simply because you've never talked with them personally before." There was no weariness in his comment—only a cheerful resolve that that is what he was paid to do.

Later, in interviewing the miners that worked for him, I was impressed that every one of them cited him as their chief communication source about the mine and the company. There were over two hundred employees at that site, and they all saw him as the one to go to when you wanted straight information. Their reasons were simple: he tells the truth, and he respects you. In focus group after focus group with the miners, the story was the same. Equally interesting was the fact that despite the company's tough reputation for demanding results in an industry in turmoil, I have never seen such a spirit of teamwork and mutual respect in a work team. Miner after miner said the same thing: "This is the best group of people I have ever worked with. We all know one another's jobs, and we all help one another maintain productivity and make this mine successful. We can beat any coal mine in Appalachia in our production, despite the fact that the natural coal conditions here are among the least favorable of anywhere in the country. Roger [the mine boss] is the reason."

As I listened, I was reminded again of the magic of good face-to-face communication practiced conscientiously and consistently by a person who sincerely cares about both results and people. Which raises an interesting question: can you put someone into a leadership position whose personality is the opposite of Roger's and get what the model says it takes? My experience tells me that it is far easier to select the Rogers of the world in the first place than to try to make a good communicator out of someone who simply lacks the skills and the conviction.

The ones who are perhaps constitutionally unable to carry it off are those who in their heart of hearts have little regard for or trust in the human spirit. For them, even the practice of learned techniques falls short as they perform without conviction the methods they have been taught. Today, the audience is smarter, more sophisticated, and perhaps more skeptical than ever before. The best answer is to select the right people and turn them loose with the right training and development and ongoing support.

If you think of the likely results of creating a more positive work climate where most people are willingly asking, How can I help? you will have something akin to the climate that exists in a volunteer organization. It is fascinating how much energy and talent volunteer organizations can command by virtue of the teamwork and initiative they inspire. Rarely in such circumstances do you hear people object that "that's not my job." Instead, they take on willingly what they would otherwise regard as menial tasks in support of the cause. The difference between such organizations and the workplace is that people are there because of their commitment to a common cause and a common vision.

The manager who can create a similar kind of climate in his or her work organization will find a long list of personal payoffs. People will require less supervision. They will feel a greater sense of teamwork and cooperation. Morale and commitment levels will tend to be higher. The group members will often settle conflicts among themselves. Individuals will be more flexible and less likely to resist change. They will be more productive individually and collectively and will pay greater attention to the quality of their work. It is an important list of payoffs for anyone who is leading a work group.

After years of seeing all kinds of organizations, I can almost smell the difference when I enter a reception area, an office, or a factory. In the oppressed organization, the atmosphere is repressive and almost snarly as people resentfully go about their business. In the well-led organization, there is a spirit of achievement, pride, and helpfulness. People seem more relaxed and more satisfied with themselves and with their work. They even smile more and go out of their way to help.

The difference for the workforce when they are led by enabling managers comes in large payoffs. For one thing, the enabling manager or supervisor is their primary information source, which is exactly what the research tells us they want. There is a perceived alignment between their work contributions and the organization's goals and outcomes, and therefore there is meaning in their work. They feel a greater sense of job focus. They also feel valued and listened to as respected members of the organization. They have a better understanding of the big picture, and they exude a greater sense of being part of a high-performing work group.

For a company that is in the right business, that understands its marketplace, and that strategizes effectively, such workers are the single most precious resource for ensuring the company's success. They are indeed the human capital of that organization.

Chapter Six

Telling and Retelling:
The Leader's Communication Role

One of the most interesting roles in any organization is that of the boss. People are intrigued with power and its uses, so it should be no surprise that there is intense curiosity about what it means to be the top dog. Some years ago I interviewed then Xerox CEO Peter McColough for the company newspaper. He told Joe Varilla, the lead interviewer and corporate head of internal communications, and me a story that typifies how people often react to the mood and whim of the boss.

McColough had made a casual remark to someone a few weeks earlier about the drapes in his comfortable headquarters office in Stamford, Connecticut. The next thing he knew, they were missing. When he asked if they had been sent out for cleaning, he was informed that someone had ordered them replaced, at what he thought to be an exorbitant cost. The incident surprised him and reminded him that he had to be careful about what he said to whom and when.

An even more outrageous example, in a vein similar to the drapery incident, was once related to me by a colleague in another Fortune 50 company about one of America's most famous and admired CEOs. It seems that a long-service employee was kept on the payroll at corporate headquarters to run errands and generally to serve as the company gopher. When the new CEO wondered aloud one day who this guy was and why he was employed for such tasks, the gentleman was quietly offered an early retirement package and sent packing.

Several weeks later the CEO casually inquired after the old fellow who used to run company errands. He was horrified when he was informed that he had been retired early because people thought the CEO was upset about having such a person on the payroll. "Why the hell would you think a thing like that?" he demanded. "I never said that. Get him back!" As the story goes, it took quite a lot of persuasion to convince the new retiree that he was indeed again welcome as a headquarters employee.

The moral in both stories is that senior leaders are powerful influencers and need to be careful about the signals they send. The subtext is that in their desire to please, people close to the power in an organization often are too literal in their readings of the mood and whims of the boss.

The CEO of the Twenty-First Century

The sending of unintended messages aside, what the key communication role of the CEO should be is one of the more pressing questions in today's emerging organizations. Peter Drucker has maintained consistently through many decades of writing and thinking on the subject that the "distinctive organ of organizations is management" (1994, p. 72). He has long argued that the senior manager's primary responsibility is to think through the theory of his or her business and to identify the assumptions on which the organization should base its actions. I would agree, but I would also emphasize the obvious: if those assumptions are not clearly and emphatically communicated to the people who have to do the work, there will be little application of those understandings to the work to be done. Most observers agree that Drucker is right when he asserts that the contemporary organization will be run by what he calls "knowledge workers"—people who use their knowledge and skills to achieve an organization's goals.

In a knowledge organization, the assets ride the elevators. Those assets must be carefully cultivated and nurtured if the organization is to succeed. The emerging role of the CEO in the twenty-first-century organization has much to do with the cultivation of such human assets.

Drucker has long maintained that management is not a bundle of techniques—perhaps the most damaging fallacy endured by the modern organization—as people tried to separate and manage discrete functions in the hope that excellence in each function would yield excellence for the whole. The truth is that today the CEO and other senior leaders must be thoughtful people who understand how to integrate disparate functions to make the organization productive in the service of a customer.

CEOs are a critical part of this effort; but to suggest that they can single-handedly carry out this monumental task is nonsense. They must be the tone setters, the people who keep everyone else focused, and the keepers of the value system. To achieve their goals, they must also be experts in managing the various systems that comprise the organization. My personal quarrel with much of what I have seen in my work through the years is that senior leaders have presumed that communication was an incidental process, that it did not have to be managed like the organization's other management systems, that it was a matter of creating fast and efficient channels through which information could move without sufficient regard for the creation and clarity of the message, much less for the strategy of the process.

Making communication a management system with an emphasis on strategy and message content, accountability for process outcomes, and training for the task is the real challenge. Seeing communication programs as merely channels to distribute information rather than as ends in themselves is the required mind-set. In too many organizations such programs take on a life of their own, and the task of the communication people is to tend the existing programs without regard for their relevancy or their value. Many years ago I heard communication expert David Berlo warn an audience of communication professionals that if they did not step up to the problem of connecting the communication process to the leadership process, they would become an organizational anachronism. He claimed that the "computer programmers" (as they were then called) were ready to fill the void with technology solutions. His words were prophetic, as in the intervening years, we have become more intrigued with the possibilities of information highways in cyberspace than we have with human information needs in what really are corporate communities. For my money, too often the technology solutions simply become another set of programs whose existence convinces the leadership they are communicating effectively.

Drucker says it succinctly: "In all organizations managers need both the knowledge of management as work and discipline and the knowledge and understanding of the organization itself—its purposes, its values, its environment and markets, its core competencies. . . . The essence of management is to make knowledges productive. *Management, in other words, is a social function.* And in its practice, management is truly a liberal art" (1994, p. 72; italics added).

A CEO Communication Model

David Pincus, an author and the director of the M.B.A. program at the University of Arkansas at Fayetteville, has made the study of CEOs and their communication roles a specialty. In his book *Top Dog* (1994) he offers a behavioral prescription for the communication role of CEOs in what he calls his CCOS model. The first C stands for *consistency*. Like most observers, he says that it is critical for the top leader to be consistent in both words and actions. The Say-Do requirement is particularly critical for top leaders, who too often find themselves trapped between their pronouncements— their announced intentions—and their contradictory actions.

His second C stands for *compassion*. Pincus makes the point that a good leader must listen to the feedback from the workforce and show some sensitivity for the plight of the people he or she is leading. Compassion does not mean that the leader refuses to take tough actions when they are necessary, but rather that he or she weighs consequences and tries to inflict as little pain as possible in taking those actions. Some would argue that compassion gets in the way of leadership, but without compassion the leader is no more than an unfeeling dictator and the organization an indifferent and even a cruel place.

The O in the Pincus model is for *organization*. Here Pincus cites the need for the CEO to think carefully about his or her communication role and to strategize what it should be in a very deliberate way. I would agree with Drucker that in practice this means that the CEO must be an interpreter and analyst of the business realities the organization faces. In the private sector, that means talking about such powerful market forces as competition, globalization, the need for cost effectiveness, and the impact of technology. It also means translating what those forces require of the organization and how they shape overall strategy and priorities. In the public sector, it means identifying why the organization exists in the first place and who it must serve if it is going to survive. It also means connecting the organization's priorities to the need to serve its stated public purpose. Much of today's antagonism toward government stems from an inability to articulate such things both to the people who pay for the service and to the people who provide it. The easiest thing in the world is for a public organization to turn into a self-serving bureaucracy; it is a clear and ever present danger for those in public service. The public-sector leader needs to be constantly communicating both inside and outside the organization to keep it honest and to rationalize its work.

Visions as Visual Aids

When I wrote earlier of the power of visions in organizations, I had in mind the CEO as chief visionary. Jack Welch at General Electric (GE) is one of the prime examples of what I mean. Early in his career as CEO when he was working diligently to refocus the company, he made it absolutely clear that GE was going to be in a limited number of core businesses and that each of its entries into the marketplace would be either number one or number two in its marketplace. If it could not maintain that position, then GE would divest the business in question and invest its resources elsewhere. This is a vision and a direction that is crystal clear in its directness and simplicity. It is also a vision that Welch pursued consistently and rigorously with splendid market results.

Welch has always been willing to spend whatever time was necessary to explain himself and to clarify to GE people why the vision is so important and what it means in day-to-day operating practices. His personal appearances at GE's Crotonville management development center are legendary. He asks the program participants to offer their questions and challenges without hesitation or fear. Many CEOs would delegate such appearances to underlings, but Welch clearly sees his communication role as one of the most critical pieces of his job.

Pincus claims that the CEO also needs to be *selective* in how and when he uses his communication power. Hence the final S in his CCOS model. Pincus reasons that if the CEO spends communication capital too freely, there is a loss of impact when something important needs to be said. It is a worthwhile point so long as selectivity does not deteriorate into invisibility.

A hazard of the leader's job in the modern work organization is becoming trapped in the office. The late Sam Walton, who created the modern empire that is Walmart, thought that a day in the office was mostly a day wasted. His objective was to spend as much time as he possibly could out in the stores meeting employees and customers. He had learned long ago that the office was the place that trapped him and isolated him from the realities of his business.

Another major problem for CEOs and senior leaders is the actual trappings of their offices. I have spent a fair amount of time in plush corporate offices with their thick carpets, rich wood paneling, and spacious work spaces filled with expensive furnishings, costly paintings, and staff people ready to serve every possible need of the boss. It is an unreal environment designed to feed egos and to remind people of the high station they have worked so hard to reach. It is also an environment that can and does intimidate the visitor. Think of the employee thrust into such an environment and expected to look past all of the trappings and tell the senior person the truth about much of anything. All of the signals suggest that here is a person of power and authority who is used to hearing what he wants to hear, not what he ought to hear. Much of that impression is accidental and unintentional, but it nonetheless works subtly and directly to discourage honesty and candor.

Wise senior leaders will emulate the Sam Waltons of the world and leave this environment at every opportunity in favor of the everyday world where their workforce labors. If they don't, they run the serious risk of hearing only what people believe they want to hear.

Four Key Communication Leadership Tasks

The modern CEO has at least four key communication roles to fulfill if he or she is to lead successfully. One is that of *myth teller*, by which he or she keeps alive the heroic tales of the organization. Every enterprise has its mythic heroes who did the right thing at the right time to guarantee the organization's well-being. The CEO should know who these characters were in both the ancient and the recent history of the organization. They serve as invaluable role models for the kinds of virtues the organization needs to perpetuate, and the CEO needs to talk about them.

After I worked at Xerox, I was a vice president for Towers, Perrin, Forster & Crosby, the well-known international consulting organization. At their new employee orientations they always featured a presentation by Chuck Root, a retired ex-manager who knew the four founders personally and who could recount homely and even semioutrageous tales of their various virtues and peculiarities. It was the highlight of the three- or four-day session to hear him hold forth on their exploits and accomplishments and make them real for the people who knew them only as names on a letterhead. It was mythmaking at its best and a practice I would commend to every CEO as a means of humanizing what otherwise often seems to be an inhumane institution.

Good communication is often good storytelling, making something come to life and making it something to which one wants to dedicate one's energies or even a career. Even today at Xerox, the late Joe Wilson is remembered as not only the founder of the modern organization but as a mythic character who embodied a caring spirit that made the organization different. I presume that the stories of his legendary ability to remember people by their first names and to offer them his common touch are still told. I have an indelible image of Wilson, truly an aristocrat and a millionaire several times over, on the day of Martin Luther King's funeral leading the parade of both black and white mourners through downtown Rochester as an expression of his sincere sympathy and compassion for the loss of a great leader. Such role-modeling and statements of a value should never be lost. In large measure, it is the CEO's job to keep them alive.

A second communication role for the CEO is that of *motivator*. He or she needs to be the chief cheerleader for the organization. The research on employees shows clearly that they want to see and hear their leaders. In fact, senior leaders in most organizations typically rank only second to supervisors as the preferred information source in the organization. Unfortunately, when people's actual information sources are surveyed, the senior leaders generally rank almost at the bottom of the list. In far too many organizations they are names in an annual report or in boxes on an organization chart. Of all the gaps between preferred and actual sources indicated in the research, this one is the single largest in terms of reality versus expectation.

When the top management of an organization engages in personal motivation by appearing in person at company meetings, they can do remarkable things. The late Mike Walsh, when he was CEO of Union Pacific and leading a transformation in the business from a typical railroad operation to a company in the transportation business, decided to hold what he called "town meetings" at Union Pacific locations throughout the United States. He would gather a group of hardened railroaders together in a local meeting place and offer them a no-holds-barred opportunity to come listen to his plans and to ask any question they liked.

In the early going some of the meetings were pretty heated and vocal, with accusations flying back and forth. But little by little, he managed to bring the bulk of employees around to his way of thinking. It was quite an accomplishment for a nonrailroad man to convince an audience of railroaders that they had to become a transportation company, that the railroad business would ultimately lead them down the road to bankruptcy and extinction.

Not incidentally, it was also a neat piece of role modeling for the rest of his managers, none of whom could now claim not to have the time for such discussions since the boss himself had found ample time in his crowded schedule. Which brings us to the third part of the CEO's communication job description—that of *tone setter*. He or she has to be very careful about personal behavior and personal ethics. The "don't do as I do but do as I say" approach will not work in the modern organization. No one can preach cost-effectiveness and cost control and then make an exception of himself or herself. The cynicism engendered by Roger Smith of General Motors (GM), when he exited in 1990 with a $1.2 million dollar a year retirement at a time when GM was losing money was a bitter pill for most GM employees (Ingrassia and White, 1994, pp. 20–22).

In addition to opulent perks and highly inflated compensation packages, the other communication trap for CEOs is trying to defend the indefensible. It would have been easy, though certainly ill advised, for James Burke, CEO of Johnson and Johnson at the time of the Tylenol crisis to claim no responsibility when the product was contaminated in a series of bizarre product tamperings. Instead, he instituted a recall of Tylenol capsules and implored the public not to use the capsules until the problem was solved. Certainly every employee in the company was given a clear lesson in how to deal ethically with a very painful problem as well as in what constitutes responsible communication.

The final role of the CEO as communicator is what I would call *"keeper of the human climate."* While this task bears a resemblance to that of tone setter, there is a difference. It requires the CEO to be the person to take the longer view of the impact of company policy, practice, or one scheme or another. There is often a tendency in organizations toward the Watergate phenomenon. By that I mean that sometimes someone at a senior level proposes what is at bottom a stupid idea, but no one has the courage to tell him that it's really dumb. If just one of the Watergate conspirators had had the guts to challenge the first person who said, "I think that we should break into Democratic headquarters and try to discredit their campaign by stealing campaign strategy"— or whatever was said at that first meeting in which the scheme was born—there would have been no Watergate scandal. The problem is that the Nixon administration had no one—including especially its CEO—who was willing to play the role of keeper of the human climate.

I recall one episode in consulting with a large organization in which the most senior person in the human resources function was offering a particularly unenlightened policy for the consideration of the CEO. The author of the policy had the full support and cooperation of his fellow staffers as he presented the scheme to the CEO for his consideration. After listening politely, the CEO turned to the people he paid to concoct human resource policy and said in no uncertain terms that he could not believe they were seriously offering a scheme so contrary to the best interests of the workforce. He then proceeded to remind them of their roles as advocates for employees. It was an interesting moment, to say the least. The CEO played the role that the human resources staff should have been playing, but fortunately he was prepared to set the correct tone for the organization.

Getting Through

In addition to the four tasks just discussed, the CEO also needs to be the organization's primary agent for change. Good leadership means that the leader is constantly studying the marketplace and its shifting character. Both he and his senior leaders need to be expert observers of the shifting sands of that marketplace so that they can describe the new landscape and what it will require of the organization's membership.

In this regard, it is especially important that all senior leaders understand the character of change and the ability of people to understand and absorb change. In a world in which it is essential for organizations to respond quickly, even sometimes in order to survive, there is a great temptation to be impatient, to demand quick results. That temptation is something the CEO in particular must keep in check as he or she reminds people of the victories they have achieved together and the progress they are making.

The continuing question of senior leaders is: How can we get through to people? How can we get them to understand things in the same terms we do? The question, of course, is specious. There is no way that employees in hierarchies can see things in the same terms the boss does. He has more information, more to lose, and more monetary and psychic investment.

Similarly, it is difficult for the boss to put himself in the same position as the people he leads. But there certainly are things that he can do to close the gap. He can be more tolerant of people's natural reluctance to change until they understand what the change implies for their lives. He can recognize that organizational transformations always lead to some degree of chaos in the short term and that he must help people cope with that chaos by keeping them focused on a vision. He can admit that he does not have all the answers and that he and the employees will learn together as they try to invent the organization they need for the twenty-first century. And he can develop a renewed respect for the democratic values we have been brought up with in western society.

This issue of democratic values is pivotal. The changes we must undergo in the workplace to make work organizations more effective require the active participation of the workforce. That participation simply will not happen unless people are actively encouraged to contribute through solid communication practices.

American workers have long been conditioned to a dictatorial world in which they have been expected to take orders and to wait for someone else to take the initiative. That conditioning is very powerful. So, suddenly empowering them to do otherwise is a trickier proposition than it first appears. Leaders at all levels will have to convince people that they are serious about wanting real employee participation, that honest mistakes will not be punished, and that they as leaders care about the people they lead. That means that leaders will have to put greater faith and trust than they generally have shown in human nature and in the desire of people to do their best at work.

Author and consultant Marvin Weisbord says it all in *Productive Workplaces* (1987, pp. 378–379). He admits that

> democracy is a tough way to live. With all its flaws, it beats the alternatives. I do not wish to have someone else, no matter how educated, well-intentioned, wealthy or wise, decide unilaterally what is best for me. Unless we are deeply involved in our work, we cannot feel good about ourselves. Unless we work with others toward valued goals, we cannot infuse hope and aspiration in our lives. Unless we treat one another as equals, we cannot find dignity, meaning, and

community in our work. Unless we make our own mistakes, and learn to forgive ourselves, we cannot learn at all. Unless we cooperate, we cannot survive. . . .

The conceptual tools exist. Our motivation was never higher. Our methods need to be bolder. Getting everybody improving whole systems is the new road map, a legacy our great grandchildren richly deserve. More to the point, it is the only one they are likely to find worth inheriting.

Chapter Seven

Challenges to Effective Strategic Communication

Reactive communication is a simpler solution to the task of organizational communication than is strategic communication. Reporting news is a straightforward process. Developing effective communication strategy and executing it well is a much more challenging task, in my opinion.

The shape and character of organizations are changing from the old, hierarchical chain-of-command structure to something much flatter, much more organic in character, and certainly much more dynamic. The purpose of hierarchy is order. The purpose of the new organizational forms is to provide organizations that are hospitable to cross-functional collaboration and to mustering people and resources quickly to serve customer needs.

The orientation of the new-age organization is more horizontal than vertical, more collaborative than individualistic, and more fluid than rigid. Understanding and accommodating the customer's needs have shifted the communication focus in organizations from a vertical to a horizontal perspective.

The Challenge of Horizontal Communication

Yet I would maintain that the single most difficult kind of communication to strategize is horizontal communication—the flow of information across organizational boundary lines. The reason is not hard to find. As I have already said, the traditional organization is characterized by hierarchy, authority, and vertical power.

In hierarchies, those who occupy the top positions have a vertical sphere of influence. The authority of their positions extends downward. Therefore, the flow of information in a hierarchical organization has typically been top-down and bottom-up. The senior person has not had much power laterally other than what he or she can exert simply by being a senior officer in the organization, and that power typically has had much to do with reputation or charisma or a kind of command presence.

For most of my working career I have heard the admonition that the cardinal sin is not to respect the chain of command. Workers have been advised not only to keep important information inside their function or department but also to move that information methodically from one level to the next, in practice respecting the power of the manager at their level to alter or kill the message if he or she chose to do so. The phenomenon of the frozen middle—through which no information passes in organizations—owes its existence to the indulgence granted to middle managers to "spin" or even to kill messages if they do not like them. This phenomenon is still very much a reality in far too many work organizations despite recent attempts to change it.

If information going down and up a vertical organizational path faces this kind of scrutiny and potential distortion at each level, think how much more difficult it is to send it horizontally, where traditionally there has been no particular obligation to keep anyone informed other than the need for occasional collaboration, temporary work alliances, or simple courtesy. In fact, in many instances the expectation is either stated or implied that you should not transmit important information across organizational boundaries except on a "need to know" basis. That does not mean that the system is not full of leaks. The employee grapevine has always been the back alley of information exchange in command-and-control organizations.

Of all of the changes that have come to the modern work organization in the last decade or so, few are more significant than the flattening and streamlining of corporate bureaucracies. In an effort to make organizations leaner and more responsive to customers, American business has made unprecedented changes. The result is that there are fewer middle managers and supervisors than there used to be, and there certainly are far fewer workers to carry the workload.

Some senior managers will admit in their unguarded moments that their companies had a long and arrogant tradition of "get the product out"—not caring much what customers thought but building what they themselves believed the market needed. The task of Sales was to unload this stuff on a "take it or leave it" basis. When there were no global competitors in the boom years after World War II, it was possible for a good many American companies to get away with this cavalier attitude toward customers.

But beginning in the 1970s and 1980s, the game changed. Quality producers in Europe and in Asia finally forced the hands of American producers and in many cases drove them out of their market niches. When losses in market share became serious, the American companies had to change their ways and learn how to apply the total quality process and principles of customer service to fight off the aggressive and efficient global competitors encroaching on "their territory."

Challenging the Silo Mentality

In today's information-based organization, a good communication process is the lubricant that keeps the organization running. Effectively serving a customer necessitates a horizontal rather than a vertical flow of information. As Figure 7.1 illustrates, practically any process that can be identified to create and sustain customer service and satisfaction is bound to cross a number of functional boundary lines.

Still, the dominant organizational structure today is vertical and hierarchical, and whether we like it or not, organizational silos—

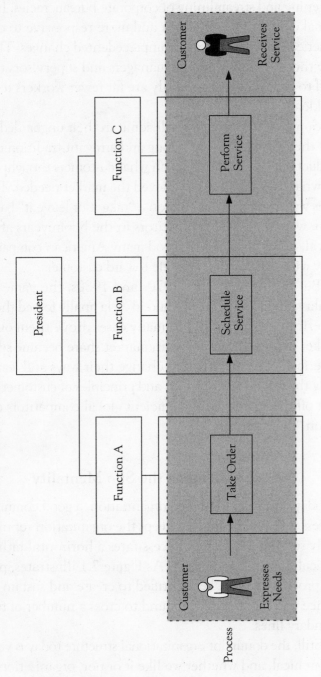

Figure 7.1. Cross-Functional Cooperation to Meet Customer Needs.

those vertical edifices that define authority and "turf" boundaries and block the horizontal flow of information and cooperation— remain a fact of life in most workplaces. The question is how to break down the silo mentality that continues to impede both team- work and the horizontal flow of information. By imposing territor- ial interests on work processes and focusing people's energies upward rather than outward to the marketplace, silos also thwart the orga- nization's responsiveness to changing customer expectations and demands.

The most important starting point for facilitating the flow of information horizontally is the individuals who sit on top of the various silos. Their example, their shared focus, their ability to work with one another, and their continued insistence that the whole is more important than any parts of the organization are crit- ical. As a consultant, I am always concerned when I interview the members of a senior staff and discover that they do not talk to one another about key business issues and values and that they may even disagree fundamentally about the direction and strategy of the business.

It is not surprising that there can be disagreements and con- flict on a senior staff, especially during times of uncharted change. What should be of concern is when those disagreements do not get aired and resolved, and when there is a lack of common direction and commitment to common goals. It is imperative that the senior staff function as leadership role models and that they make it their business to insist on collaboration among the organization's func- tions. Their influence as communication role models in this regard is profound.

The creation of multifunctional teams to identify and address sticky problems is one way to facilitate communication across boundary lines. But such teams do not come together spontaneously and naturally. Their members need to learn over time to trust one another, to share information freely, and to confront and resolve their conflicts constructively. All of that can certainly happen within the right climate and with the right chemistry on the team, but it is not a simple matter by any means.

Perhaps more than anything else, team members need to understand how to align their efforts with the corporate vision and the missions and objectives of other teams so that their end products are compatible with those developed by other teams. The behavior that is required is relatively new to most organizations, which have operated on the basis of independent functions whose efforts presumably came together automatically in the overall strategy and plan for the business.

While we can pretend that team members naturally find their leadership within the group and spontaneously understand their roles, that is a dangerous assumption at best. Someone in the team must take on the role of leader and address the six questions about human needs outlined in Chapter Five. If that kind of leadership is not provided for or does not somehow arise out of the team itself, team members will become mired in their frustration and lack of direction, not to mention their lack of solid accomplishment.

Forming Natural Alliances

The encouragement of alliance building and networking across boundary lines is also an important strategy for minimizing the impact of silos. Ad hoc work groups organized according to common interests and objectives and linked together purposefully are the most productive organizational structures imaginable. They work because people working in a common cause tend to share information naturally and spontaneously in their efforts to achieve mutually agreed upon goals.

When the Saturn organization was formed to build a new GM car to compete with the Japanese automakers and other small car producers, it was organized not by vertical departments but by multifunctional teams of people responsible for the separate subsystems that would finally make up the car. It was clear to each team that their role was to produce the best subsystem they could and to integrate their work with that of all the other teams.

Some of the early going was not easy, since people brought their old cultural baggage with them to the new organization, which was designed to be collaborative and which featured joint management by GM and the United Auto Workers. But the pressure was on to produce a superior low-cost car. The final product is a tribute to the people who worked through the early problems and challenges of collaboration and who learned how to overcome their varied corporate experiences and biases in their dedication to common goals. No one can quarrel with the ultimate quality of what they produced together using the power of dedicated teams and good joint leadership from senior management and the union.

The quality of information sharing across boundary lines is generally a product of the culture of the organization. In win-lose cultures, this is a very tough issue indeed because the boundary lines are forever in dispute and the game becomes how to fix and harden them to your adversary's disadvantage for as long as possible. Conflict becomes a matter of one group imposing its will on another. In more collaborative cultures, where people are fixed on common goals, the emphasis is on win-win, with all sides trying to seek solutions that each can live with and that ensure that they can continue to work together effectively. In today's process-oriented organization, the latter style is obviously an imperative.

Total Quality as Transformation

The most encouraging operational solution to date to the problem of cross-functional communication has been the total quality process with its emphasis on the primacy of process and the effectiveness of integrating whole systems in the pursuit of quality, customer service, and continuous improvement. If you want to improve quality, the quality gurus have taught us, work on the continuous improvement of all of the key processes that combine to create a product or service. Engineer those properly, create enabling organizational structures that facilitate and encourage teamwork, drive fear out of the organization and give people the power to make decisions, and then provide them with a way to measure their effectiveness. Without the total quality process and the focus and discipline it brought to the Saturn project, it is doubtful that the car would have been the ultimate success it has turned out to be.

But total quality is not a quick fix. It takes massive doses of open communication and behavioral change to make it work. When it is properly applied to any organization, it changes that organization and the way it operates in fundamental ways. Sheila Sheinberg, an expert on change management and quality, says that her word for what we must do is not change but transformation. She believes that what we need is a revolution in the way we do things. It is a tough message for naturally conservative organizational leaders to swallow, but readily allowing that these are dangerous times for organizations, Sheinberg argues that not seeking transformations is really the most dangerous course of all.

Her view is that organizations must heed all of the signals that tell them they must change—not in small ways but even before it is clear that "the ground is shifting beneath their feet." The problem is that when leaders acknowledge that massive change is necessary they face the painful fact that both they and the organization will enter a period of confusion and chaos, that for some time they will be building bridges between the old and new ways and leading their people across those bridges.

In regard to that concern, CEO Jack Welch of General Electric has been quoted as saying that anyone who is not confused today simply does not understand the problem. The difficulty is that the mythology says that leadership confusion means leadership weakness and incapability to deal with problems, so we tend to bluff. Unfortunately, bluffing often leads to lying—to others and even to ourselves.

In the vertical organization, the obvious task is to find out how to promote the communication of not just information but of truth across vertical boundary lines. Those who stand on the boundaries in organizations are in some ways in the most precarious positions of all. There are no maps or compasses to guide them as they seek to invent new organizational forms and solutions and to encourage cooperation and teamwork from people who are perhaps more accustomed to being rivals in the competition for scarce organizational resources.

Resistance to Change

Perhaps the most comprehensive attack so far on traditional organizational practices of all kinds has come from the reengineers. Their objective has been to foment the revolution Sheinberg advocates. Process change, structural change, and most important, the elimination of anything or anyone that does not add value to the organization's products are all fair game.

The reengineering experts have confessed in recent times that they are surprised at the extent of the resistance to change that they have found in organizations. They lament that the task is even more difficult than they had bargained for; they are hired to create new ways of doing things and new ways of looking at the business, only to find that there is often a vocal—or worse, a subtle and passively resistant—opposition to their proposals.

Frankly, I am surprised that they are surprised. When Price Waterhouse LLP conducted a survey of the reengineering efforts of Fortune 500 Industrial and Fortune 500 Service companies, they found that companies have had far greater success in cutting costs through reengineering than they have had in increasing revenues.

The Price Waterhouse people found that only 41 percent of the service companies had reengineered their human resource practices—particularly performance measurement and compensation tactics—

that directly affect human behavior. Seemingly, the majority of the companies were attempting to change their process behavior without changing structures or the ways in which they led and rewarded people. Certainly, if we continue to reward and promote the functional identities and interests of the silo organization, it stands to reason that we will have little horizontal cooperation or communication.

Especially interesting is the finding that the typical reengineering emphasis on cost cutting has increased internal resistance to change because employees fear the consequences. Contrariwise, they will embrace the opportunity to increase revenues because it is a more positive, hopeful initiative than cutting costs, which feels like retreat and withdrawal. Employee involvement and open communication across boundary lines are critical to this more positive approach, Price Waterhouse claims.

Significantly, of the companies that were most successful in overcoming resistance to their reengineering efforts, 100 percent cited good communication as a factor that helped them achieve their goals. Factors in the 90 percent range were strong mandate by senior management (95 percent), setting up intermediate goals and deadlines (95 percent), and having an adaptive plan (91 percent).

Price Waterhouse's conclusion was that if companies fail to overcome human resistance to change, "reengineering will continue to deliver benefits only on the cost-savings side of the equation. Revenue gains will be small, and reengineering will prove to be a technique of only modest value" (Dauphinais and Bailey, 1994).

Setting the Climate for Change

In Sheinberg's view the new organization must fit Warren Bennis's well-known vision of an adhocracy—teams of people who come together to accomplish specific tasks and then disband and reformulate to tackle new projects. Such an organization is closer to a biological model, reforming and adapting itself to meet the challenges that come at it constantly.

Hierarchies and bureaucracies certainly appear too rigid to take on the long-term challenges of today's marketplace. But it is unlikely that we will soon see their demise. Because they have the ability to impose a felt sense of order and control in the workplace in the midst of the chaos and confusion that change brings, they will likely endure. The man on the white horse is still an attractive image when ambiguity reigns. I believe that most likely in the near term at least we will have to settle for ways to minimize the rigidity of hierarchy and create innovative techniques to ensure the adaptability of the work team.

Some hints about how to go about this process come from the work of Alan Schnur, senior vice president of human resources for the Robert Mondavi Winery and a former consultant and employee opinion researcher. Over many years Schnur has amassed data that speak eloquently to the performance differences of high-performing and low-performing organizations. He believes that in the end organizations induce people by their systems and behavior to make choices about how they will or will not perform. In his work he has managed to isolate some critical performance factors, most having to do with communication strategy and practices (Schnur, 1995).

The high-performing organizations in Schnur's sample were selected on the basis of three criteria: they had to have been profitable for the last three years before their inclusion in the sample, they had to operate in a truly competitive market, and they could not have been bought or sold in recent years. The high-performing companies were then compared with a group of poorer-performing companies in the sample, as determined by their operating results. The attitudes and behavior of the hundreds of thousands of employees in the two sets of samples were then compared. The results were startling, not so much because there were great surprises but because the contrasts between the employees in the two types of organizations were so vivid.

In the top-performing companies, accurate and timely communication was considered essential. Input was solicited from employees at all levels in setting direction and policy. Competitive advantages and barriers to success in the marketplace were also discussed regularly. The rationale for change was communicated when important changes were being made. Both good news and bad news was moved quickly—and safely—through the organization. And senior management fostered an ongoing dialogue with employees. In a very real sense, the leaders opened the books to their employees.

Specifically, in both the top-performing companies and the poorer-performing companies people were asked if they knew of ways to improve their department's efficiency. In both cases more than 90 percent said yes. In the high-performing companies 74 percent said that their manager or supervisor regularly asked for their ideas for improving efficiency. In the poorer-performing companies only 41 percent said that they were asked by their supervisors to supply such information. In Schnur's words, "Statistically, that is a quantum difference in behavior. The poorer-performing companies teach people to keep their mouths shut."

I have seen exactly the same phenomenon in my own work. Not surprisingly, people in poorer-performing companies read this failure to ask for their opinions as a devaluing of their worth. Not to be asked is to be seen as not counting. The typical employee comment—especially from blue-collar people—is, "They think we're too dumb to have any ideas worth listening to." For their part, knowledge workers are more likely to express their feelings of frustration in apathy and cynicism that lead to loss of commitment and, as they readily admit, lost productivity.

The unfavorable contrasts hold right down the line. On the issue of "having enough information to do my job well," 79 percent agree in the high-performing companies, 52 percent in the poorer-performing companies. On "having appropriate authority/ discretion delegated to them" (read "empowerment"), 89 percent agree in the high-performing companies, 55 percent in the poorer-performing companies (Schnur, 1995).

Some people would like to put a reverse spin on such information and argue that the results are some kind of halo effect—that the high performance creates positive attitudes. To some extent, that is true. Members of winning organizations feel much better than members of organizations that are losing. But Schnur says that his data show clearly that there is no correlation between performance and employee satisfaction or morale. Some very satisfied people still do lousy work, and whole organizations can feel good and still be among the poor performers. In Schnur's view the top-performing organization gives people the opportunity to do good work, and taking advantage of that opportunity is what makes the organization and its people succeed. His view is that people make choices about their behavior at work and that those choices determine who wins.

It is hard to argue with his logic from any practical observations I have made through the years. People in high-performing companies act and talk so differently than people in poorer-performing companies that you cannot help but be impressed by their spirit and energy when you are in their presence. And you cannot help but notice that this spirit and energy is translated into deliberate work choices to collaborate, to share information, and to participate as a team player. The silo may still be there, but people move in and out of that silo freely and seldom see it as an organizational barrier to cooperation, interaction, and information sharing.

The Dark Side

The dark side of organization life, I would maintain, is the misuse of power and the abuse and devaluation of people. There is obviously nothing wrong with hierarchical structures per se. Some of them are very effective and even efficient in their ability to concentrate solutions on serious problems. In an emergency there is no substitute for a strong authority figure who can mobilize people to action.

But most of organizational life is not an emergency. It is an effort to lead people in the accomplishment of group objectives in support of the organization's larger objectives. It calls for teamwork and integration of individual and group efforts. It calls for the exchange of information regardless of personal egos or agendas, and it therefore calls for open communication without fear of personal consequences.

In hierarchies, we have often seen information distorted to serve the ambitions and needs of powerful people whose main interest is the preservation of their power. In short, the culture has too often been designed—deliberately or not—to serve the needs of the leaders rather than the needs of the people. It may sound like the most conventional wisdom to say that today this has to change, but we are struggling mightily as we try to make those kinds of changes and to rid ourselves of this dark side of organizational life. So, it is likely that the transition will be uneven, chaotic, incomplete, and longer in coming than we can afford.

Orchestrating the Strategy

So far I have been talking about the fairly straightforward issue of communication roles in an organization—that of the leadership, the staff functions that assist the leadership, and the managers and supervisors in their day-to-day communication responsibilities. Stated in that fashion, it all sounds rather simple and orderly. I do this, we do that, and you do that. But the *real* challenge is integration—putting it all together so that everyone in the organization is aligned behind a set of clearly understood goals.

The process is a bit analogous to an orchestra. While each member may be a proficient musician, nothing truly musical happens until everyone is playing from the same score. Also, the orchestra cannot be led effectively by the first trumpeter from his chair in the brass section. Someone has to step up and take responsibility for choosing the music, leading the tempo, and starting and stopping together.

Alternatively, the orchestra can turn itself into a group of self-managed performers, but the result will more closely resemble improvised jazz than it will a symphony. Or the brass section can form a brass quintet. Or the strings can isolate themselves into a string ensemble. A few musicians might buy some amplifiers and play a little rock and roll. But in each case, the separate result will be very different from the full sound of the orchestra with its disciplined leadership and arranged effort.

I don't want to belabor the point, but organizational communication is a lot like that. It does need to be orchestrated if it is not to turn into improvised solos or noisy disharmony. The leadership has the role and responsibility of initiating and monitoring the process and for the ultimate outcome, not to mention for providing the motivation and the will to keep at it. Staff specialists need to contribute their particular points of view, support, and talents. And all employees have to participate in some cooperative fashion based on their self-interests and their interest in successful outcomes.

Communication can and must be horizontal as well as bottom-up and top-down, but the leadership must be like the orchestra leader in arranging, leading, and responding to the flow of the music. Staff specialists, despite their dedication and talent, cannot lead from their sometimes-isolated positions in the organization. And individual employees or groups of employees cannot be expected to pursue much more than their own perceived set of interests unless someone persuades them to commit to a common, worthwhile vision and mission.

The need I propose here, to orchestrate communication, to some extent flies in the face of an emerging viewpoint about organizational communication that I would call—for want of a better term—the empowerment paradox. Empowerment is a great concept in a democratic society. It says simply that we will give people the power to make decisions and to take responsibility for those decisions. It comes from the notion that customers ought to be served by reasonable people who have the latitude to make decisions in the customers' best interests. It tries very hard to free people from overly restrictive policies and bureaucratic approvals and to create satisfied customers. So far, so good.

For people to be empowered, they clearly need information. Good decision making has always required good information. That in turn means that people must have free access to whatever tools can provide them with information. It also means that they must be free to consult with whoever in the organization has the information they require. Here we begin to come into practical conflict with the historical ways in which organizations have done business.

The command-and-control style of management has been more deeply entrenched in business than in most other types of organizations. I suspect the reason is the number of World War II veterans who rose to positions of authority after the war and brought this style of leadership to their new jobs. Now we are saying to people, in effect, don't worry about all of that chain-of-command business. Go get the information you need when you need it. The extremists in this discussion are saying, forget about trying to manage information. Just open the doors and let people help themselves. They will instinctively serve each other's needs and create organic, workable information systems. If you want empowered people, you must have an unfettered communication system. And oh, by the way, with the new technology and with broad access to that technology, you really don't have any choice anyway.

In the legitimate interest of empowerment, the extremists are happy to live with communication disorder, chaos, and unpredictability. In fact, they welcome it as a breath of fresh air when compared with the old tendencies toward secrecy and information control. If the choice is that clear, it is hard to argue with their position. But the joker here is the very real problem of information

overload and the potential misuse of technology. The ability to produce information has exploded exponentially in our society in the
last decade or two. Personal computers, desktop publishing systems,
laser printers, E-mail, voice mail, and fax machines have all per-
mitted anyone who wants to be a publisher of information to
indulge his or her fondest wishes. But while the production of
information has advanced light years, the consumption of information is just as slow and costly as it was when the printing press
was first invented. Whether you are reading a page on a computer
screen or a printed page like this one, whether you are listening to
a message on voice mail or viewing it in two dimensions on a television screen, *the human cost* of hearing, reading, and perceiving a
given message is constant. It is just as high in contemporary times
as it was in the Reformation.

At what point do people become so burdened with messages
that they shut down to them? No one knows yet. Watch people in
airports and other public places. Cellular phones, laptop computers, paging devices, and the like often control their movement.
There is practically no place to hide from information, and the situation will certainly get worse as the years go by. Every space will
potentially become a work space. And every worker will be wired
into some kind of communication network. It is a scary prospect
that in many forms is already with us. In this evolving scenario, at
what point does empowerment slip into enslavement?

I have always believed in a sort of Gresham's Law of communication. The essence of the original Gresham's Law in economic theory is that bad money drives out good money. In effect, cheap
money will chase out money that is backed by gold or other solid
assets. Similarly, I believe that bad communication drives out good
communication. In other words, to the extent that we overload
people with junk messages, we lose the opportunity to connect with
them with important messages.

A friend reminds me that there are two ways to deny people information. The obvious one is secrecy and control. The less

obvious one is to deluge them with every scrap of information so that they can no longer separate what is important from what is merely interesting from what is junk.

I have no solution to this question other than the one I have already posed—namely, making communication a strategized, market-based system with the appropriate accountabilities. But I worry about our ability to do this as one of our major challenges in the twenty-first century. I believe that the best antidote is the one I have proposed here—that and the intelligent use of communication technology.

Jeffrey Hallett, chairman of the Present Future Group, is more optimistic on this issue than I am. He claims that the senior managers of any organization will have to recognize management information systems as the pivotal tool in moving the organization forward. In his words, "the move toward empowered employees and team-based management will bring about a new set of mutually supportive relationships between the organization and its members" Hallett, 1994, pp. 14–16). The challenge, he says, is a suitable communication strategy, which he concludes will become the communication craft of the future.

Communication Strategy Roles: Leaders and Staffers

Leaders must accept the responsibility for making the communication process a true management system with a strategy, accountability, and education and training. If people need information as the raw material for performing their jobs, it is management's responsibility to see that they get it—or at least have access to it. As with any raw material, it must be of high quality, it must be there when it is needed, and it must be processed in such a way that each person who handles it adds value to what he or she has received. In my view, that means a deliberate and well-managed process and not the haphazard movement of unorganized raw information.

I do not mean to suggest that information should be censored and access to it tightly controlled as it has sometimes been in the past. What I do mean is that leaders should be worrying about the overall efficacy and efficiency of information flow in their organizations. They would not neglect the efficient flow of other kinds of raw material in their manufacturing processes because they understand that the costs of such neglect are unacceptable. So, if information is a raw material today, why are we not spending more time worrying about how it is being processed and handled to produce value-added results?

Do people have a market-based understanding of their work? Have they been told of the priorities of the business and why those priorities exist? Do they understand the measures that determine whether the business is or is not succeeding? Are they being treated like capable partners in an important undertaking in which their effort is crucial? In the end, are they able to use the powerful information tools at their disposal to improve their productivity and their contributions? That's the real measure. The vital leadership communication role is to ensure that these questions are properly addressed by all levels of leadership.

It is in the formulation of communication strategy, which Hallett calls the communication craft of the future, that leaders must join forces with the people inside and outside the organization who can best assist them. Otherwise, I believe, the disorder, chaos, and unpredictability of both technology and changing organizational cultures will worsen the confusion of change and leave people more at sea than they already are.

No one can say precisely what form this collaboration should take in a particular organization. In the best case it will be an alliance of the CEO, the human resource leadership, the communication professionals, and the information systems people. Whatever form it takes, the real need is for a carefully conceived communication strategy that is rooted in the needs of the customer, the needs of the marketplace, and the logic that the marketplace can bring to bear on otherwise confusing organizational actions and developments.

I believe that in this alliance the communication professionals need to play the lead role in worrying about the clarity of messages and the all-important issues of context, vision, and the linkage and alignment of messages. To the extent that the change process is necessarily messy and ambiguous, the communication people must work constantly to rationalize it with the perspective of the marketplace. Senior leaders, human resource people, and communication people currently need to work very hard at the process of self-reinvention and renewal as well as the process of nondefensive collaboration—by which I simply mean putting the whole above their parochial interest, biases, and personal agendas.

Sorting It Out

More than anything else, the unresolved issues reported here reflect the difficulties in moving away from old structures and forms in response to essential change. The new structures are still merely working outlines of the future. The exciting challenge still ahead is to determine how best to make those structures work and how to connect people in processes and networks that enhance the efficient flow of information inside and outside an organization. The eventual solution, I believe, will have much to do with the alignment of corporate vision, business objectives, and individual effort. It will also have much to do with good, solid leadership from people who recognize the primacy of human capital to the organization's success and who understand how to connect marketplace demands and human effort.

However we finally do it, one thing is clear: our ability to make those connections will largely determine our success or failure in a global, information-dependent economy. The companies that do not learn how to turn all forms of internal communication into a well strategized, accountable process with its roots in the marketplace and a vision derived from market possibilities and hope will be the also-rans—or worse—of the information age.

Chapter Eight

The Importance of Trust

In the beginning of this book I said that there was a better way for organizations to communicate with their people. Lest you have become lost in the details and the collateral issues as we have made this journey, let me now try to sum up what I believe are the essential elements of that better way—what have lately come to be called "best practices."

One of my least favorite questions about internal communications is Who does it right? What's the company we should be visiting to find out the secrets of good communication with the workforce? I can't provide a simple answer to that question because I do not at this point see any company that really does it all right. A major reason for that is the unprecedented challenges now being faced by modern institutional organizations. Another reason, as I have already emphasized, is the weight of tradition and the fears of those who do not want to change, all of which are heavy anchors that hold companies back in their efforts to change.

The reengineers, to their sorrow, have been hit head on by this resistance. Anyone who has ever attempted to counsel senior management on the issues of change knows that people claim they want to change the way they do business and the wasteful behavior that affects their bottom lines. But those same counselors will be quick to tell you that they find themselves surrounded by the naysayers on all sides when they try to help institute real change efforts.

The alcoholic may swear to you that he wants to stop drinking, but rarely does he fully understand the grip the bottle has on him and his life. So it is with organizations. They may swear they want to change and they may put into place all sorts of initiatives to make it happen—only to discover that the past has a fatal attraction when they must come to grips with real behavior change.

One of the great pluses of the old days was its unshakable optimism and the faith that people had in future growth. I remember years ago at General Electric when a senior executive was stopped in midsentence as he was expounding the bright financial future of his department in front of a group of his superiors. The country was in the grip of a recession and he was asked how he could be so optimistic when the economy was so bad. His surprised response was, "I have always been taught that the curve only goes up at GE."

The present age suffers from an opposite disease that makes real change all the more unsettling and the past all the more fondly remembered. The danger of the unfolding vision of the information age is that it will project such a bleak picture of the future that no one will want to go there. Reengineered, downsized organizations with everyone giving his or her last gasp of energy for the cause are not an attractive vision. They may inspire sufficient fear and insecurity to keep people on their toes for a time, but there is no excitement in mere survival. As one veteran of the downsizing wars in a major corporation said, "Don't try to scare me anymore. If you're going to shoot me, do it and get it over with."

Best Practice

Back to my original point: does anyone "do" communication right? The answer is yes. Their names are always on the honor roll of enlightened companies and in the lists of best companies to work for. You know them well: 3M, Xerox, Hewlett-Packard, FedEx, Apple, Microsoft, UNUM, Merck, and others. Ironically, if you were to tell that to the employees of most of the companies on such lists, they would look at you with mild to strong surprise, even skepticism. That does not mean that they are ingrates or whiners. They are heavily invested insiders with a basis of comparison between management's words and actions. Many of them would readily agree with the outsider's assessments if they were making external comparisons.

In those cases where employees would readily agree, there are some common elements worth noting. First, no matter how rudimentary or inelegant the strategy for communicating with or leading people, it is usually well articulated and easily identifiable with clear accountabilities spelled out all around. For example, CEO Jim Orr at UNUM says that along with communicating the vision and other business issues, the leadership makes every effort to tell people important company news as quickly and fully as they possibly can. His logic is that this willingness to share information freely and quickly promotes trust and a sense of inclusion.

The companies that communicate well also tend to have visible leaders who see communication as the most important element of their jobs. At Hewlett-Packard, for example, coffee talks—informal question and answer sessions between leaders and their employees—are an institution, as are all-hands meetings—more-formal briefing sessions by the boss.

Companies like Hewlett-Packard and UNUM also respect people's right to know about the things that affect their jobs and their lives. They may worry about outside pressures and perceptions, but they know that it does little good to please outsiders if in the process you alienate the people who must deliver the product or the service. It is a tough balancing act to deliver honest and timely internal communications when there is an adversarial press out there and an equally adversarial group of financial analysts waiting to take apart your every statement. But the good companies find a way to strike the necessary balance and to keep their people well informed about company issues and events before they get the news from the public media.

The company leadership that cares about its internal communication efforts crafts messages with great concern for clarity and timeliness as well as sensitivity to people's ability to absorb what they are getting. It also allows people to respond and to ventilate their concerns. Further, it listens well and responds appropriately. Roger, the mine manager I quoted in Chapter Five, said it best: "You're on trial every morning. It takes weeks, months—even years—to win trust. But you can lose it in a second . . . and it takes forever to win it back."

Communication in Demoralized Organizations

As a consultant, I typically get to spend more time with dysfunctional organizations than I do with progressive ones. Roger was right on the money. Once trust is lost on a wholesale level, the communication task becomes almost impossible.

I have found that demoralized workforces usually have some things in common. First, they suffer from a lack of direction and a sense that the organization is not dealing with systemic problems they regard as evident. More often than not, it is official silence about company problems that leads them to this conclusion. The organization leadership that opts for silence in the face of turmoil is playing a high-stakes game. People will invent their own explanations, and they will not be pretty.

The second characteristic of demoralized organizations is that somewhere in the past the leadership has acted in a less than forthright fashion toward its own workforce. The action may have been blatant, like a dramatic and surprise downsizing. It may have been the sudden removal of key figures without explanation, giving rise to the belief that it is treacherous at the top, and only the devious survive. It can be the institution of arbitrary and sometimes small practices and policies the workforce sees as harassment.

But the greatest cause of demoralization I see in companies is the sense that leaders have abdicated their leadership responsibilities and are not dealing with serious market issues. People will eventually get over a downsizing, although they may have trouble with their guilt and fears about surviving. But they have the most difficulty handling a sense that the organization is leaderless. It is at that point that they resort to conspiratorial theories or fears that the Three Stooges are running things.

The most difficult business client is the one who has insufficient capacity to act on its problems. A memorable example for me was a health care organization where the doctors exerted their collective power to block their leadership from dealing with the significant problems the organization was facing in its marketplace and in its internal operations. The doctors were more interested in preserving their power and their perks than they were in addressing the organization's market issues. In the end they stymied their own leadership and sacrificed the interests of the rest of the workforce to their personal privilege and desire to retain the status quo.

Still another example was the old-line company where the leadership kept the workforce in the dark as well as in a kind of subjugation. The CEO was a man everyone regarded as brilliant but ruthless and manipulative. He made matters worse by rarely visiting field operations and by permitting people to make up an even more sinister persona for him. The word on him, even among his top lieutenants, was that he was bright but you never knew what he was going to do, that his personality was mercurial. In selecting leaders in the company's decentralized operations, he typically picked the people he could control and who would continue his hard-nosed policies with the workforce. To say that the workers were demoralized is an understatement.

And then there was the automotive plant manager who delighted in surprise inspections of the lockers his workers used to store their belongings. In a search for contraband and petty pilferage, he would send his security people to saw off the locks, confiscate whatever they found—including forbidden coffee pots and the like—and fire the transgressor. Another of his favorite practices was to deny overtime to anyone who drove a car he thought exceeded their station at the plant. The stories of his arbitrary firings of people were legion. The last word on this man, who was eventually fired by a new general manager after years of abuse, was spoken by one of his supervisors in a focus group: "You know the difference between our plant manager and Hitler?" he asked me without a trace of humor. "He lacks Hitler's warmth and compassion." No one laughed.

Such examples may sound like a throwback to another era, but they are still very much with us in companies whose names might surprise you. I have long since concluded that the issue of capacity and willingness to act is the critical one in helping to create constructive change. So long as people in leadership positions fight to preserve the status quo and decline to be open and forthright in company communication—particularly in the admission and definition of marketplace issues—I think there is little hope of real change or of improving the communication climate. Roger said it all: it takes forever to win back trust once you have lost it.

Human Capital and Human Resource Policies

In an era in which the human capital of an organization is one of its primary assets, it is imperative to nurture and develop those assets with great care. Formerly, in the old manufacturing organizations that used to dominate our economy, people were simply another cost of doing business. Today, in a service economy, they are literally the means of doing business. That shift is monumental. It is particularly important for an organization that has reduced its workforce to the point that it is highly vulnerable to lapses in human productivity and commitment.

We need to do better with our human resource strategies. For one thing, the reward system in many organizations is now out of synch with the organization's objectives and priorities. In the old days, it promoted and rewarded individual effort. Today we need team effort in support of coordinated processes. Yet, most companies continue to rely on individual merit pay programs tied to individual performance appraisals as the backbone of their compensation systems.

Likewise, development and training efforts need work. Reengineering guru Michael Hammer told the *Wall Street Journal* in an interview that we need different kinds of managers from the ones we have created in the past. In his view, three types of skills are needed. He says, "One I call a process owner. It's really a work engineer, who's concerned about how we go about filling work orders, designing products. The second is a coach—teaching, developing people. The third kind is the leader, who primarily motivates—creates an environment where people get it done. Hardly any of our existing managers have any ability to do any of those things, or the inclination" (Lancaster, 1995, p. B4).

I would agree. But I would take it all back to three earlier questions—What's my job? How am I doing? Does anyone care?—and the need to deal with each question as a human issue in the new work organization. We clearly need to develop people who can lead based on those understandings.

Hammer goes on to talk about development in these terms:

> I tell companies they need to quintuple their investment in education. Training is about skills; education is about understanding broad knowledge. Everybody who works in a company needs to understand the business. You go into a factory or warehouse and start asking some rudimentary questions: Who are our major competitors? What is our strategic vision for the next five years? If you're serious about reengineering, they have to understand the business to understand why they're doing it and how they're going to have to operate in the aftermath" [p. B4].

Hammer's colleague, James Champy, adds, "These are things that need to be taught in the company context, both through classes and experientially. We want workers to make decisions, and they can't do that without a business context" (p. B4). Which is precisely the point of this book.

Declining Employee Loyalty

Employees have had some bad things done to them in recent years to make them less loyal, less trusting, and less confident than they used to be. A lot of the fundamental change that organizations have undertaken has been at the expense of their workforces. No one can deny that much of this was essential, but a lot of it was also opportunistic. It is much easier to make massive cutbacks when everyone else is doing it. The justification to outsiders is practically self-evident. Indeed, the security analysts lick their chops, it seems, every time one of the major companies announces a downsizing.

The extent of the damage that has been done to work relationships was shown in a study financed by fifteen major companies, including the likes of American Express, AT&T, Sears, Xerox, and DuPont (Shellenbarger, 1993). In a sampling of some three thousand wage and salaried workers, the Families and Work Institute found that those surveyed expressed greater commitment to their jobs than to their employers. Almost 60 percent strongly agreed with the statement, "I always try to do my job well, no matter what it takes." Only 28 percent said that they were willing to work harder to make their companies succeed. The final picture is of a workforce that, not surprisingly, has little loyalty to employers and also is deeply divided by race and gender—a fact that does not augur well for the future of communication or teamwork at work. With so many women now in the workforce, it was also disheartening to see the extent to which they did not see bright futures for themselves. Women managers in particular were twice as likely as men to rate their career advancement as poor or fair.

What was perhaps most striking in the study was that employees said that they placed the highest value on the quality of their work environment. In fact, *the single thing they considered the most valuable in looking for an employer was open communication in the workplace.* Two thirds of the sample cited that value as very important. The next three items in order of importance were the effect of work on one's family and personal life, the nature of the work itself, and the quality of management at work.

The clear implication is that the employers of the twenty-first century who figure out how to address such issues will have a much greater chance of rekindling declining employee commitment. Especially attractive were such workplace benefits as flexible scheduling or the right to work at home to achieve a better balance between job and personal life.

The Necessity of Accountability

Regardless of workplace arrangements, one thing is clear: the communication process in an organization must become a deliberately strategized management system. There must be accountability for communication behavior, and if that accountability is to be real, the organization must provide the education and training to make it fair.

The best of systems or strategies mean little if there is no accountability for people's behavior. I am still amazed at the number of work organizations that develop solid communication plans and permit managers at all levels to choose not to participate. Would they tolerate a manager who declined to submit a budget for his or her operation on the grounds that such documents are inhibiting to their style? Would they accept the argument that the manager has no time for such activities as financial discipline? That her regular duties keep her so busy that she cannot find the hours to manage a budget? I doubt it.

Would an organization permit people not to submit annual goals and commit to attaining them? Of course not. But the same organization will tolerate managers and other leaders who beg off their communication responsibilities by pleading lack of time or discomfort. Like my old friend the jaded sales manager who complained that he was only as good as his last thirty days' performance, they are allowed to get away with the claim that they have other

priorities. What leadership priority could possibly be more important than informing and leading the people under your direction?

Most of my emphasis on accountability here is on leaders and
managers. I do so deliberately because they have traditionally been
the larger part of both the problem and the solution. But what of
the average workers in an organization? What about their communication responsibilities?

I think the answer is obvious. Their responsibility is to communicate openly and without the selective filtering that people often
engage in at work. But—and this is a crucial but—that requires high
trust and an environment in which there is little or no fear factor.
In too many cases the history of work organizations has been marred
by distrust and subtle and not so subtle repercussions. If we are to
create organizations that function on the basis of the free exchange
of information, they must be free of consequences for speaking one's
views openly and responsibly. Or as W. Edwards Deming, the guru
of quality used to put it, we must drive fear out of the organization.

Caveat Emptor

At the same time, the responsibility of the individual employee is
to be a wise consumer of work information. There is a "buyer
beware" clause in much of what I say here. In recent years, with all
of the downsizing and the need to reduce costs, some employers
have resorted to policies and practices that border on exploitation.
In many places, people are expected routinely to work fifteen or
twenty hours or more over a normal forty-hour work week without
additional compensation or consideration of their needs. Because
American business has been in a low-growth cycle in recent years,
people have accepted such demands and have taken the extra time
from their personal lives because the message they get from their
leaders is, "If you don't like it here, there are plenty of others we can
get to do your job."

It is an unhealthy situation for all concerned. Employees burn
out and suffer fatigue that can only hurt their performance on the

job. The social consequences for child care and for not having the time to tend to normal family responsibilities are increasingly obvious in U.S. society. Ultimately, many people ask themselves if the price they are paying is worth it as they find themselves exhausted, economically strained, and with a marginal quality of life.

Until the employers who behave in an exploitative fashion deal humanely with this problem, I believe that the people who work for them have to maintain portable skills and protect themselves against unscrupulous work practices. Historically, people have always done this quietly by keeping their own counsel and leaving a job when they judged it was time to do something more suitable or to find other ways to make a living.

But there is a serious loss all around when people feel they must protect themselves against employers who do not respect their needs or their dignity. In recent years especially we have seen talented women leave promising careers where there was no respect for their needs. At the same time we have also seen talented young graduates shy away from more traditional employment to begin their own enterprises. It is a talent drain we cannot afford to ignore.

While it is far from the complete answer, I believe that an important part of the solution is simply good leadership from everyone, from the CEO to supervisors. There are at least three parts to this need. One, we have to begin making it absolutely clear that effective communication behavior comes with the management territory, that it is the means for doing the job. Two, we have to provide people with the information and the incentive to perform their communication responsibilities. An important part of that incentive is to offer clear guidelines for the behavior so that there is no mistake about expectations. And three (probably the most effective answer), we need to *select, recognize, and reward* the supervisors, team leaders, and managers who do this job well.

Closely related to the question of incentives is the matter of training and development. Not everyone is comfortable in his or her communication role. We have to make it clear that good communication practices are as important as any of the other job priorities people face, and we have to give people whatever skills training they lack. Are they poor listeners? Teach them how. Do they have few platform skills? Give them courses in effective presentation. Do they not understand how to handle and resolve conflict? Teach them. Are they clueless about coaching other people? Show them how. There is nothing that difficult about the skills training task. It is only a matter of assigning it a priority in the workplace and making sure it happens.

The Macro/Micro Issue

What is perhaps most difficult about the issues I have examined in this book is that they operate at two levels. Every organization has its big-picture, macrocommunication issues that people need to understand so they can better manage their jobs. At the same time, the work reality they live with is normally restricted and confined. This reality has much to do with a work unit, a diverse collection of co-workers, and a boss who has tremendous influence over day-to-day events and day-to-day experience. I would estimate that 90 percent of the communication issues in an organization are at this microlevel. Address those needs, and most of the personal communication problems go away. Ignore those needs, and the communication issues increasingly become major barriers to effectiveness and human productivity.

Still, the macrocommunication issues are also critical. How do people understand their roles in the organization if they do not understand the objectives and priorities of that organization? The answer is an orchestrated communication effort at both the macro- and microcommunication levels—surely not an easy task. In the twenty-first-century organization, *someone* had better be worrying and planning about how the macro- and microcommunication activities come together. So far, organizations have generally been better at managing macrocommunication than they have microcommunication, which they have tended to leave mainly to the good intentions and varied skills of managers and workers. In an information-rich organization, that had better change if people do not want communication anarchy.

Where Timelines Fear to Go

One of the questions anxious clients sometimes pose is, "How long will it take for us to change our communication strategy?" It is a good question, and I wish that I had a good answer. Much depends on how effectively the leadership can assemble the people who will have to work together to invent and implement the strategy. In an organization that feels the need is urgent and that has the capacity to act, some remarkable results can be achieved in as little as a year. The change process will go on for a long time to come, but at least there is evidence of both changing practices and changing employee attitudes.

In those organizations that are more deliberate and that need to negotiate such changes, the effort can take as long as three to five years before there are really visible results—and even those will tend to be uneven.

Where the leadership loses its will, gets lost in the ambiguities of change, and focuses more on the stress of the process, the organization will probably never see worthwhile results because it will revert to more comfortable and known behaviors. In the process it is likely that more harm than good will be done to the communication process because of dashed expectations. The final lesson is clear: do not begin such efforts unless you are deadly serious about seeing them through to a successful conclusion.

A Single Reality

The one clear fact about all of the change we are seeing—whether it is the change from domestic to global competition, the shift from manufacturing to knowledge work, the emphasis on the customer and service to the customer, the quality movement, the streamlining of work organizations, or the changes in the way work is done and where and how it is done—is that it is all of one piece!

Such changes are a *single* reality, not a series of separate happenings. They are interwoven pieces in a connected chain. Global competition has caused companies to manufacture their products in countries with cheaper and more plentiful labor. The fear of losing business to aggressive global competitors has caused those same companies to look for every imaginable cost saving to protect their market share, their profitability, and even their viability. In turn, the attempt to cut costs has led to increased automation, the need for fewer workers to put out the same or more work, and increased attention to efficient work processes. At the same time, domestic organizations under the pressures of this same efficient competition have had to pay much more attention to their customers and their demands for quality products and services.

With employees as a primary capital asset, the leadership of such companies has had to begin to learn how to manage in very different ways. So far, they have not done a good job of educating their people to the realities of competition. What education has taken place has often been the result of the harsh lessons doled out by leadership actions taken to avert crisis. Employees read those lessons as separate, mean-spirited attacks on their welfare unless they have been schooled in the new competitive realities. The best answer to educating them to these realities is market-based strategic communication that shows the connections not only between forces and events but the connections we need to forge to one another if we are to thrive together in this uncharted new world.

So, I close with the argument with which I began: we are in the midst of unprecedented change in work organizations—breakpoint change, if you will. Communication is an essential tool for accomplishing change, but it is a tool organizational leaders use poorly or thoughtlessly. When it is used poorly, it confuses people. It also makes them angry and feeds their skepticism and cynicism, making them evermore resistant to change.

There is a far better way, which I call market-based strategic communication. Let's get on with it before it's too late.

References

Bridges, W. "The End of the Job." *Fortune*, September 19, 1994.

Bridges, W. *Job Shift*. New York: Addison-Wesley, 1994.

Dauphinais, B., and Bailey, G. "Reengineering for Revenue: New Perspectives on Creating Shareholder Value." A Price Waterhouse LLP publication. New York: Price Waterhouse, 1994.

Drucker, P. "The Age of Social Transformation." *Atlantic Monthly*, November 1994, pp. 53–80.

Hallett, J. "New Technology Redefines the Role and Importance of Business Communication." *International Association of Business Communicators Leadership Dialogue*, 1994, *1*(2), pp. 1–18.

Ingrassia, P., and White, J. B. *Comeback: The Rise and Fall of the American Automobile Industry*. New York: Simon & Schuster, 1994.

Kearns, D. T., and Nadler, D. A. *Prophets in the Dark: How Xerox Reinvented Itself and Beat Back the Japanese*. New York: HarperBusiness, 1992.

Lancaster, H. "Managers Beware: You're Not Ready for Tomorrow's Jobs." *Wall Street Journal*, January 25, 1995, p. B4.

Land, G., and Jarman, B. *Breakpoint and Beyond: Mastering the Future Today*. New York: HarperBusiness, 1992.

Pincus, D. *Top Dog*. New York: McGraw-Hill, 1994.

Schnur, A. "Communications in a Dynamic Environment." Presentation to the San Francisco Academy: session on internal communications in organizations, Seal Beach, California, January 21, 1995.

Shellenbarger, S. "Work-Force Study Finds Loyalty is Weak, Divisions of Race and Gender Are Deep." *Wall Street Journal*, September 3, 1993, pp. B1–B2.

Tichy, N., and Charan, R. "The CEO as Coach: An Interview with AlliedSignal's Lawrence A. Bossidy." *Harvard Business Review*, Mar.–Apr. 1995, pp. 68–78.

Weisbord, M. R. *Productive Workplaces: Organizing and Managing for Dignity, Meaning, and Community*. San Francisco: Jossey-Bass, 1987.

Index

A

Accountability: establishing, 99–101; and trust, 141, 147–148

All-Purpose Gas and Electric: market-based strategic communication at, 52–54, 59; reactive communication at, 31–36, 37, 40–41

Allied Signal, market-based strategic communication at, 56–57

American Express, and employee loyalty, 146

Anger, as reaction to change, 21, 29–30

Apple, and best practice, 140

Arkansas, University of, 108

Assessment, organizational: of issues to be communicated, 67–72; results of, 64–72; in strategic communication model, 60–63

AT&T, and employee loyalty, 146

Authority, in management, 89–90, 92, 101

B

Bailey, G., 128

Belief, by managers, 101–102

Bennis, W., 128

Berlo, D., 107–108

Best practices: researching, 63–64; and trust, 140–142

Bossidy, L., 56–57

Bridges, W., 80, 82, 84

Burke, J., 113–114

Business issues: and market forces, 68–70; messages of, 74

C

CEOs. See Leaders

Champy, J., 145

Change: agents for, 115–117; background on, 1–2; as breakpoint, 14, 152; burning platform theory of, 56; case made for, 59; climate setting for, 128–131; conclusion on, 2–4; and connections, 4–5, 13–27; customer as cause of, 1–12, 70–71; employee responses to, 21–22; good news on, 7–10; in nature of work, 80–99; openness to, 22; and organizations, 14–22, 119–138; rate of, 8–9, 151; and reconnections, 26–27; resistance to, 8, 127–128, 139–140; as single reality, 151–152; stages in responding to, 19–21; as transformation, 125–127

Churchill, W., 65

Communication: audience surveys for, 46–47; audit of programs for, 63; best practices in, 63–64, 140–142; conclusion on, 3; and connections, 5; of context, 49; CCOS model of, 108–110; in demoralized organizations, 142–144; face-to-face, 31, 102; Gresham's Law of, 135; horizontal, 119–121; incentives for, 149–150; issues in, 48; leader's role in, 105–117, 136–138; as management system, 49–50, 107–108, 147–148; in natural alliances, 124–125; process-focused, 9–10, 50; purpose of, 3; as strategic process, 48–52; tasks of, 111–115; and total quality transformations, 125–127; and trust, 139–152; as valued, 146. *See also* Market-based strategic communication; Reactive communication; Strategic communication

Communication professionals, responsibilities of, 6, 74

Compassion, in communication, 108–109